I STILL BUY
GREEN BANANAS

Reflections on
Living and Dying in our
Culture of Denial

By
ROGER W. HITE, PhD

Dedication

To Joyce Osternig—a friend forever.

Also by Roger W. Hite

The Return to Marlboro (2010)*
Unwrapping Christmas (2009)*
Last Stop Before Paradise (2009)*
The Marlboro Incident (2009)*
Buster's View (2009)*
The Loser ((2008)*
Buster's Spirit (2008)*
The Iron Butterfly (2008)*
Nesting Among Ducks (2008)*
Cottage by the Sea (2007)*
The Foul Game (2007)
The Five Dollar Fortune (2006)
Vivid Imagination (2005)
The Sister Deal (2004)
The God Switch (2004)
Soul Merchants (2004)
Buster's View (2002)
Mirror Man (2001)
Buster Back at the Wall (2001)
The Twelve Candle Miracle (1999)
What's the Good Word? (1999)
The Ebony Snowflake (1999)
The Art of Awe (1998)
Our Gift (1998)
Buster at My Side (1997)
Buster at the Gate (1995)
Buster at the Wall (1994)

*Still In Print

PREFACE

Life is about death. Death is about life. There is no honest way to understand one without seeing the other—unless, of course we do what many of us learn to do and live in a culture of denial. Such a culture diverts awareness away from death and hides its everyday presence.

Unfortunately, (or fortunately, depending on one's perspective) a time comes when we must set aside denial and confront death. I am at such a point once again in my own life's journey.

I am writing this book to help me through the grieving process of dealing with a close friend's terminal disease. I started this introspective journey while she was receiving medical treatment and continued to write it when she entered hospice and the end-stage of her disease. She died on June 14, 2010.

This collection of reflections makes no pretense to add any new insights or theories that will benefit the academic discipline of thanatology.

My reasons are personal and self-serving. I want my wife, my sons, my grandchildren, my brothers and sister and my close friends and associates to have a written record of what I think about death. Why? Sometimes in the future I will die and no longer be with them. I want

4

them to know my views now while I am living—perhaps out of the belief it will make my own passing easier on all of us when that day arrives.

I have not been diagnosed with a life-threatening condition. I am not morbidly preoccupied with thoughts of death. To the contrary, I have a fierce optimistic passion for living.

At the age of 66 I still buy green bananas and plan future vacations! I relish each day. I enjoy a loving marriage relationship and a host of friends and neighbors. I enjoy the time I spend each day in my study creating fiction and writing about non-fiction topics I think matter.

I've been blessed with good health and have had only one serious encounter with a life-threatening situation. A few years back a physician friend and colleague performed an angioplasty on me and inserted two tiny stents that opened my 100% occluded right coronary artery. Had my condition gone untreated I would not be sitting here writing this book.

The night before my procedure I thought a lot about death and dying. It was for me a real possibility I had given little thought to during the first 60 years of my life. Even though several family and friends had died, I grieved through those experiences and then retreated into our culture of denial.

Our friend's recent death underscores for me that my own death is inevitable. I have, however, learned all the patterns of avoidance and denial most of us use to ignore such a reality. I enjoy the illusion (or delusion) death is something that happens to everybody else.

Like most of those who will read this book, I am a card-carrying citizen of this "culture of denial." It is not my purpose to explicate all the permutations of its complex patterns of denial, nor is it my goal to rescue any reader from its influence.

Thinking about death makes us sad. Thinking about living makes us happy. The plain truth is people do not like to talk about death, except when forced to deal with it in their personal circumstances.

Indeed, we treat it like the proverbial "elephant in the front room" and use dozens of euphemisms to soften the harsh reality of death.

The proof we live in a culture of denial is evidenced by the reaction many will have when they pick up this book and peruse this preface. They will initially be intrigued by my title. Once they realize I am talking about death many will return this book to the shelf and look for lighter, more cheerful subjects.

I encourage you to be brave and read on. This is not a negative or a mournful sad reading. This is a book aimed at improving one's perspective on **living**, not **dying**—but it is about creating a perspective that acknowledges we must live **WITH** death and not deny the important role it plays in the human experience.

As difficult as it is for us to talk about death in our culture of denial—it is even more difficult to suggest there are ways to view it in a positive light. Death deserves to not be personified as the grim reaper or the bad guy in the black hat.

Contrary to what I have learned through living in our culture of denial, here is the reasoning that provoked me to take another look at the concept of death.

It can be argued that without death, life as a human would have an entirely different meaning.

Pause a moment and consider this: Suppose the human condition was such we knew from the time of our birth, we would never die. Now consider our current circumstances. How would we live life differently if science or some incredible force granted us the opportunity to live forever in our human form—to not endure the aging process but to be preserved at the prime of our life forever?

What would we focus our worry on? What would be our source of a crappy day? How would we live differently?

Would we worry about retirement? Would we try to pay off our thirty-year home mortgage in fifteen-years? Would we be afraid to run up our credit if we knew we have forever to balance the books?

How humans would behave if we didn't face death can best be illustrated by how our government and national leaders think about the future. Governments are corporations designed so they legally survive a human lifespan.

A government does not view itself as a finite corpus that has a birth and an ending—perhaps if it did we would have a totally different world view. Perhaps we would develop and share resources more widely—knowing there is an end point somewhere in the future. Governments that run up huge debt, waste resources, ignore the destructive impact their decisions have on the world around them, are perfect examples of what happens when one lives under the illusion (delusion) they are going to live forever.

Sadly, a look at the world financial situation today is evidence of how our culture of denial impacts governments who suffer from the delusion of "immortality."

Instead of dealing with the ever-present reality of how bankruptcy, foreclosure, and business failure are all political equivalents to death in our socio-political-economic world, governments deny there will be a time when they will be accountability for bad decision-making.

Imagine what kind of world we would have if the billions of humans residing on this big blue marble called Earth behaved similarly to our governments in their private lives!

No thank you! Remaining forever in my human form in the current world of human enterprise is not my definition of heaven on earth!

Our finite human life is the perfect condition because of—not in spite of—the reality a human life-span ends in death!

Death is what gives value to each day and the decisions we make.

Imagine how much less a day would be worth if the currency of life was infinite? Because of death we avoid the hyper-inflation and devaluation that would occur if our days were endless.

O.K., I admit I am stretching the metaphor to illustrate what I feel about our government printing money and causing inflation as though the government were immortal and not bound by the economic laws that can and do ultimately result in financial death of a corporation.

The more we buy into the culture of denial, the easier it is for our government to behave irresponsibly and to pass forward the consequences of poor decisions.

Fortunately, we don't have to deal with this hypothetical scenario of endless life and all the chaos it would create.

But before we get on with the challenge of balancing our lop-sided negative view of death, consider another hypothetical scenario that the evolving science of genome and DNA coding has made into a reality.

We can easily imagine that even though we don't live forever, we have created the tools for knowing shortly after birth the things that will cause our demise—unless treated by medical interventions.

Given such a reality, it is easier to imagine the following hypothetical scenario: Suppose when we are born we have a date stamped on our forehead. It is like the date many food source suppliers stamp on their products—best if used before. The number, however, would be an actual expiration date. It would be our appointment with death. There would no longer be any second-guessing when we were going to "buy the farm." Everybody would know when it would be our time. It would be, excuse the pun, "as plain as the nose upon our face."

Would that change how we lived our life? If we were twenty and had an expiration date of eighty, would we take different risks? Would we gamble more on our future? Suppose we were twenty and knew our life would end at thirty? Would that make us live our remaining decade in a whole different space?

Chances are we would manage our time differently. That is why in the grand design of things we are not privy to such knowledge. Instead, we have the free-will to behave as we want. We have the free-will to make decisions as though we would live forever or as though we only have a few days left.

I think the current design is brilliant. As a Christian I consider it God's design, but I respect how non-religious can also appreciate the current design, even if they have no theological explanation for how it came to be.

The current design places the burden on us to live our lives according to what we think is important. For many, it is possible to live with death knowing that if we always do the right thing, then everything will come out in the end as it is supposed to end.

This life and death reality is compounded by the fact many humans are self-centered and compelled toward instant gratification. Under the current reality in which many suffer the natural consequences of their behavior, some of us make decisions that hasten the day when we meet our maker. Lifestyle choices—smoking, alcohol, excessive food consumption and obesity, lack of exercise, you name it—can hasten our appointment with death.

Why is a beautiful, wonderful friend afflicted with cancer and dies before her statistically predicted time? Why do people who commit terrible acts against others seem to live long after their time?

Who knows? A cynic may hypothesize good people don't know the date of their demise. Bad people do— it's some kind of cosmic code known only to the bad guys. That's why they do bad stuff to good people.

It is OK to scoff at such a theory. And it is preposterous to make such speculations. The one thing I have learned in my life experience is it doesn't make any difference how much good a person does during their life—there is no relationship or correlation with longevity.

I'm glad God created the human life experience so we have to deal with both life and death. I'm glad human life is finite and we do not know the time of our demise. I wouldn't want it any other way. I don't pretend to understand how it works but I have faith God does.

My hope is that by talking openly about my perspective of death I can help create for myself and other a healthy, balanced perspective—one that acknowledges and accepts death is a part of life.

I don't relish the thoughts of my own final days—though I hope and pray they are peaceful and pain-free days in which I share and enjoy my final moments with friends and family.

I love life so much so that even the Christian gospel's promise of an eternal after-life in the presence of God is not sufficient for me to willingly relinquish my awesome human life I currently experience.

That's the way God wired my nature.

I will behave as Dylan Thomas once encouraged his dying father to do when he wrote "Do not go gently into that sweet good-night. Rage, rage against the dying of the light."

Hopefully my energy and determination, however, will not be one of anger, but one of raging passion to squeeze every bit of life out of my dying spirit and my final days.

I am not running from death, but if it must be perceived as a contest, I would like others to say I stayed in the race to the very end. I made Death work hard to catch my spirit. I would like folks to say I relished the reality of living with death until the moment I crossed the finish line.

That's the way God made me.

My friend's death underscored for me how there is no right or wrong way to deal with death. My friend's way was a very private way. The confrontation with the reality of death is a unique human experience we each face someday.

Decades ago I helped set up the first hospice volunteer training program at Mercy Hospital in Sacramento where I was Director of Staff Development. I used a story to introduce staff to the concept of trying to understand death.

My story told of a prince who was being chased by his enemies. The prince arrived at a pauper's cottage and pleaded with the poor farmer to allow him to hide under his bed. The peasant complied.

A band of angry men soon stormed the cottage seeking the prince. The peasant held his breath as the men searched the place and stabbed their prodding spears through the bedding to make sure the prince was not in the bed. He wasn't. He was under it and could see the spears as they poked around through the straw mattress.

When the men left, the prince crawled out from under the bed. He profusely thanked the frightened peasant. He told him, "You can have any wish you want granted? Name your desire?"

The peasant trembled with relief that the prince was not discovered under his bed—knowing he would have been killed for concealing the prince.

The humble peasant thought for a moment and then said, *"I'm curious, sir. Can you please tell me what it was like—what did you think about as you saw the spears pierce the bedding? What was it like thinking you'd finally come to the end of your life?"*

The prince was taken back at such a humble request—especially when it was within his power to grant the peasant great wealth and a better fortune in his life.

The prince simply shook his head and seemingly withdrew his generous offer. He left the cottage shaking his head in disbelief.

Several days later, while the peasant was out in his front yard tending to a garden of vegetables, the prince's private guard arrived on horseback and carted the poor peasant off to prison. They said the prince was insulted by the peasant's seeming mocking of the prince's generous offer.

The hapless peasant spent the night in a dungeon and was informed that in the morning he would be hung at the gallows.

In the morning, the peasant was led to the gallows and a rope was placed around his neck. Just as the executioner was preparing to pull the lever that would open the floor and leave the peasant dangling in the noose, a horseman rode up into the courtyard. He commanded the execution be halted.

The peasant breathed a great sigh of relief. The executioner removed the noose from his neck. While that was being done, the horseman unfurled a scroll and began reading a royal letter to the trembling peasant.

"The other day when I hid under your bed to escape from my killers, the only thing you requested was knowledge of how it felt to confront the reality of one's impending death. I hope through this experience you will consider that I have paid my debt in full."

The purpose of the story was to illustrate the reality facing anyone who wanted to be a part of a hospice care team. Until we are under the bed ourselves and are experiencing the death moment, nobody else can tell us how we are going to feel. It is a private experience that will be different for each of us.

We encouraged hospice workers to not undertake the role with the expectation they would learn about how dying people feel. Instead, we taught staff to listen and support and not to judge how individuals dealt with death.

That special private moment when we must deal with the reality of our own death is made more difficult because we are raised in a culture of denial.

What do I mean by such a statement? I mean that from a very early age we are taught to avoid things that remind us of our own mortality. We treat death as though it is something that happens to everybody else. Others die in plane crashes, in automobile accidents, and receive the bad news of a terminal condition.

We feel sorry for others and we are respectful when the evening news reminds us of the passing of some famous person who made an especially important mark on our society as an entertainer, an athlete, a politician, or a religious figure. But for the most part, we get on with life and shunt thoughts of death and mortality off to those feelings we have when we experience an otherwise "crappy day."

We spend a lifetime focused on everything else except the ever presence of death in the process of growing, maturing, and approaching our own inevitable ending. We surround ourselves with material diversions—fancy cars, clothing, jewelry, expensive vacations, luxurious homes. We use the material objects to energize ourselves and pretend that acquisition of wealth and adult toys are the measure of how well we are playing life's game. We spend little time trying to understand and come to peace with the reality we are dying as we are living—a day at a time.

When we look at our own reflection in the mirror each morning we have an opportunity to observe first-hand the great paradox of our human condition. We see the face of someone who is both living and the face of someone who is dying.

Both conditions are ever-present, though as a culture we have created a mythology of denial. We use billions of dollars of cosmetics to cover up wrinkles, grey hair, and any telltale signs we are aging. We have grown accustomed to the never-ending pursuit of the mythical "fountain of youth."

Young is good; old is bad. In the culture of denial we often set aside the wisdom and awe contained in our elders and we champion the accomplishments and achievements of those "up-and-comers."

Instead of paying respect to the other face, we deceive ourselves.

"*Nonsense*," we kid ourselves into believing, *"I'm not dying. I'm living. I've never felt better. I'm in the prime of my life."*

Some will say it is unhealthy to dwell on the negative. We should always accent the positive—to which I respond with a "yes" and a "no." We should learn to live life in balance. We need to balance both into one healthy, realistic outlook on our human condition.

I am learning, however, how a happy day can include acknowledgement and respect for the ever-presence of the dying face in the mirror.

What is the difference between a "Crappy Day" and a "Happy Day?"

Perspective! It's that simple.

You get what you see. Happiness is there for you to see. You're in charge of "seeing happy." But you also have the responsibility to see the other face each day as well.

So why do we too often conclude a day in frustration, write it off as crappy, and look forward to a tomorrow when we will be more fortunate? Because we worry about things out of our control—as epitomized by our fear that death is inevitable—that's why we put such ideas out of our mind—we confuse a healthy perspective with one that successfully denies the ever-presence of this other face.

Remember the scripture, *"This is the day the Lord has created, rejoice in it!"*

How can we rejoice in a day if we look in the mirror and see the aging face of a dying person?

Perhaps we can rejoice in being honest with our real condition instead of painting on cosmetics and continuing with our popular culture of denial. Maybe we can learn to love and accept both faces.

A healthy perspective on life isn't dependent on managing the either/or approach to denying or covering up the reality of that other face.

We would all like to live in a utopian world where we everything is perfect. I hope, however, these preface remarks cause you to wonder if a life without death would actually be ideal.

Carpe Diem!

Seize the day! This day is all you will ever have! So stop looking for tomorrow when times will get better. This is as good as it gets!

"What! How can you say that? I just lost my job. I just got diagnosed with a serious disease. I'm dealing with terminal cancer. I just ended a relationship. I just got a speeding ticket. My driver's license was suspended. I broke a tooth. I got an F on an exam. Someone put a big scratch in my car's paint."

We can all add to the list of things that lead us to the conclusion we've had a crappy day—especially if we are preoccupied with a health condition that makes us more focused on the dying face than the living face.

Embrace both faces. Then get on with the business of dealing with the stuff that needs to be balanced so we can produce a happy day.

God's gift to us is a new day; our gift to God is making it into a peaceful, purposeful day, regardless of the mixture of crappy and happy stuff that is present.

19

We can't erase the reality we are both living and dying each day.

We can't change external events.

We can, however, control our beliefs, attitudes, and perceptions about what happens. We can confront the culture of denial and say good morning to both faces.

Go ahead and buy a bunch of green bananas. Seizing the day doesn't mean not also filling it with expectations for tomorrow. Just make sure you enjoy all that is good in the current day.

1

"The Good Word for the Day"

Many years ago I co-authored with two colleagues at Dominican Hospital a small book entitled **What's The Good Word?** We explored the importance of cultivating spirituality in work organizations and how to celebrate it through various rituals and traditions. We distinguished between spirituality and religion and invited people of all faiths—or those without any—to celebrate with us spirituality.

We built many of our lessons around the optimistic perspective of greeting friends and acquaintances with a salutation that required them to find a positive word to rally around for the day.

At first, such a positive question often caught folks off guard. For some it was far easier to complain and scoff. But we weren't looking for the negative. We wanted our days and our relationships to begin on a positive note. When I opened a meeting or greeted colleagues in my office or our administrative conference room I would ask the simple question: "What's the good word?" After a while, people got accustomed to my inquiry and actually gave thoughtfully considered responses.

I confess at the onset of this collection of reflections, I am an optimist. I relish life and I love interacting with family, friends, and colleagues about all the great blessings God provides all of us each day—whether we see them or not. I am impatient with pessimism. It does such damage to the human spirit.

I also confess I am not a Christian evangelist. I do not put priority on convincing others to accept my belief system as the right system. It is right for me and I share my views for others to evaluate as to whether it is right for them.

In light of my Christian optimism about death and dying, I am annoyed at the culture of denial we have created through the taboos we have place on discussing dying and how it is a part of the daily process of living.

When I retired from my hospital administrator role and we moved to Eugene, I joined the Metropolitan Rotary Club of Eugene. It is a small group of business and professional folks who in the tradition of Rotary put service above self. This group of introduced me to the idea of "happy dollars." In the tradition of Rotary, each club has the option of developing ways to assess members in playful fellowship so funds can be raised to support the various projects sponsored by the Rotary Club.

In my life as a hospital administrator I was a member of the Downtown Santa Cruz Rotary Club. It was a large club of over 150 members. We used the concept of *Detective* to celebrate achievements and milestones of club members. The rotating job of Detective was simply to do some sleuthing to find out noteworthy accomplishments fellow members of the club were doing within their community—usually things reported in the local television and newspaper media.

The Detective's report was part of the meeting in which members were playfully honored—and then fined—for accolades and accomplishments. The fines were usually modest—3-5 dollars—and only occasionally hefty to the tune of 10-15 dollars—usually depending on the magnitude of the achievement—such as a 25th year wedding anniversary or the birth of a new grandchild—as well as the ability of the member to absorb larger fines.

While I enjoyed the detective approach, it had the drawback of being dependent on the creativity and the time the individual serving as detective had to gather stuff about fellow members. The happy dollar approach was distinctively superior because it relied on individuals to stand up and voluntarily make a club contribution in honor of something in life they felt warranted acknowledgement. It was, in fact, a politically correct way to boast about something that mattered.

Not only did the fundraising device facilitate group interaction and fellowship, but it allowed club membership to learn about what was going on in the professional and personal accomplishments of members. I found it difficult not to find some reason to pay a happy dollar and celebrate something good I'd experienced in my life.

The Rotary tradition of "happy dollars" is something I likened to asking "What's the Good Word?" It is an assertion that a friend and colleague acknowledges and gives thanks for one special blessing that occurred in the day God created.

As a writer and essayist, I liked the idea of bringing the concept of happy dollars into the evening traditions of my own home. My wife shared my enthusiasm. We took an old coffee can and wrapped it with a paper cover bearing the title: Happy Day Dollars.

On many evenings we pull at least a dollar from our wallets and thoughtfully write down on a slip of paper something for which we are happy. We agreed that after sufficient funds accumulate in the can, we will spend them on something that would make others happy— perhaps a charitable donation.

It seemed like a natural segue to use the same process to build into my writing discipline some time to reflect on things I saw as positive about the days of my life. I also realized that a balanced perspective required attention be paid to how we deal successfully with the crappy things that cause us to worry and get depressed.

Even though I am a Christian and my life is driven by the optimism that is a part of Christian theology, I am not trying to evangelize my views or convince others through scriptural evidence Christianity is the only way. It is the right way for me. It is the basis of my optimistic perspective and outlook on life.

I conclude this introduction with a bit of syllogistic reasoning:

All Christians are optimists.
I am a Christian.
Therefore, I am an optimist.

Some optimists are not Christians.
I am not a Christian.
Therefore I am an optimist.

The first syllogism is valid. The second does not allow for a valid conclusion to be drawn.

As you will see in the following pages, whether you are a Christian believer or a non-Christian, it is possible to develop and maintain a healthy optimistic perspective and outlook on life. It is possible to embrace both faces we see in the morning.

I would argue, however, that it should be a lot less challenging for a Christian to use the teaching of faith to balance the crappy day experiences with the happy day events and to confront the culture of denial.

You be the judge.

2

"The Lessons of Obituaries"

Let's be honest. Even though you still buy green bananas, the older you get the more likely it is you routinely read the obituaries in your local newspaper. I consider such a reality a positive sign you are at least momentarily escaping the grips of the culture of denial. I'm willing to bet good money when you were thirty, you seldom even glanced at that page. I certainly didn't.

When we were young we look for the good and bad news in the headlines and front page stories. Then we turned to the sports page and indulged in the diversion of athletic achievements. Then we turned to local news and perhaps finished off with a survey of the business news. Our culture of denial provided us with so many more things to worry about and get excited about—and to ignore the daily drama of death and dying.

The older we become, the more difficult it is to ignore death's smiling face in the mirror each morning. I have discovered there is also a mind behind that face as well.

That's why I am compelled to scan the obituary section of our local newspaper each day. As much as we try to silence the voice of our death face, the longer we live, the more difficult it becomes.

In crafting my perspective on life I find reading obituaries is a healthy way of balancing my view of life and death.

Now that I am almost 67 and know there are more days of my life behind me than ahead, I confess I have developed a special interest in scanning the Obituary page of the Register-Guard newspaper. I consider it the face of death's daily social column.

I need to explain at the onset that my interest in death's social column is not because I am morbidly preoccupied with death. My motive is a curious blend of drivers.

When we first moved to Oregon a couple of years ago, I was struck by a newspaper story about how Oregonians were among the least affiliated with organized religion than any other state population in the US. I soon realized, however, the operative modifier was "organized" religion. Just because Oregonians elected to check the box "unaffiliated" when it came to surveys of religious preferences, it didn't mean Oregonians are not God-fearing humans or are atheists. They are just not joiners—a condition I attribute to the rugged individualism that is still reflected in many of the small rural towns across Oregon.

What I do find myself studying in the death notices and announcements is the percentage that indicates "no services are planned." Usually about 25-30 percent of the obituaries reflect this non-affiliated status. I think this statistic is reflective of the reality that Oregonians are not affiliated with organized religions.

The other thing I always consider when I read the short life history summaries is the age of each individual. For some reason I feel better when I find that most of those who are deceased are still older than my 66 years of age. I especially like it when most of the announcements indicate folks died at ages older than 80! I feel most sad when the deceased are younger than me—especially those who die in their early twenties or thirties because of accidents or cancer.

Earlier in my life I seldom read the obituaries—what an old colleague of mine referred to as "the Irish Social Page." If I did it was only after I read all other parts of the paper. Now, curiously, after the editorial page and the sports page, I turn to the obituaries. Curiously, I now read the front page and the local community news sections last? I wonder what that says about me.

Last night on the national evening news was a short story about the death of Art Linkletter—who died at age 97. I recalled with delight all the memories I had of his earlier television shows during the 1950 and 1960—The Art

Linkletter House Party and People are Funny. He was an early precursor to the entertainment and variety talk shows now made popular by Ellen DeGeneres and Opraha. He signaled the passing of the grand old times I enjoyed as a kid growing up and being introduced to the emerging genre of family television. His most famous and delightful interviews were done under the rubric "Kids Say the Darnedest Things!"

I actually appreciate the segments of the evening news honoring the passing of some great social or political icon. Somehow the passing of people who are famous and those who left great marks on our world seem to be easier to celebrate than the passage of an ordinary person who's obituary sketches a few of the highlights of accomplishments that represent the hyphen between the date of birth and the date of death.

I am always sad when I see a brief obituary and the announcement that people are not gathering for a memorial service, a celebration of life, or a funeral. I think a human life, however brief or prolonged, is worthy of a celebration at the time of death.

I don't know yet what will be printed in the newspaper or what kind of celebration will mark the passing of Joyce. But as a writer, I needed to create for her a special memorial honoring her life. It helped me work through my grieving and closure. Here is what I wrote:

In Memory of Joyce Osternig

Many who read the recent obituary announcing the death of Joyce Osternig surely gasped in disbelief!

"I had no idea she was even ill." "She looked so good the last time I saw her—she didn't say anything was wrong."

I imagine hundreds of phone calls were placed the morning after the **Register-Guard** newspaper found its way to Eugene doorsteps and stunned readers saw the announcement of her death. Joyce was survived not only by Lou—her husband of almost forty years—but she was also survived by literally thousands of people whose lives she impacted during her thirty-some year career as a popular Eugene school teacher and administrator.

Most of the people who knew Joyce would probably realized—after they got over the initial shock—that Joyce dealt with death as she lived her life—a strong, self-sufficient person who cared intensely for others and kept private things that might cause others to worry or show concern for her. In her view the presence of cancer in her body was a private matter between her and God and her husband Lou— her best-friend and constant companion.

Although I was among those very few who knew of Joyce's grave condition, I respected her determination to keep private such knowledge. I confess, though, I was sad for her because she did not allow herself to be open to the awesome number of people who would have been at her door-step wishing to show concern and support.

Perhaps the thought of having to manage so much love and outpouring of support would have been too overwhelming— and would have made it so much more difficult to bring closure to her personal affairs during her final days.

Joyce died at home surrounded by the love of her husband, her sister and other family members. Few knew of her very private struggle with cancer when it first occurred over a decade ago. She and Lou celebrated and gave thanks when the disease was temporarily overcome and they were able to continue with their active personal and professional lives. Even fewer knew of the sadness the Osternig's felt when in late 2008 the cancer returned. Despite almost a year's worth of weekly trips to Portland for aggressive medical treatments, the cancer finally took her life.

When my wife Debby and I moved to Eugene a few years ago I soon learned to appreciate how Joyce had made an awesome impact on so many people's lives. It was virtually impossible to go anywhere with Joyce without somebody stopping to greet her. It seemed like everyone either had her as a teacher or principal or was a parent who wanted to again remind her how much they appreciated the various ways she made a difference in their lives.

I was reminded of her impact when I jokingly challenged a woman at Bob Welch's writer's conference when she boasted she knew everybody in Eugene. I remember teasing her by playfully asking, "I'll bet you don't know Joyce Osternig!?" To which the woman gleefully sat up in her chair and replied, *"Joyce Osternig! Sure I do. I was a young teacher when she asked me to come to the class she was teaching at the University of Oregon dressed in my Halloween*

Costume I called the costume my' Queen o farts' outfit to demonstrate to my language arts class the importance of proof-reading! She was a great teacher! I consider her one of my mentors!"

Once we were going with the Osternig's to spend a few day at their cabin in Black Butte. We were following Lou and Joyce in our car because they had to return to Eugene for some social function that evening. We pulled off the highway to a rest area where we were going to have a picnic. No sooner did we step out of the car and head toward where the Osternig's were parked than a third car pulled into the lot. And, true to form, when the couple got out of their vehicle and spotted our group a smile beamed on the face of the woman. She came right over and proceeded to give Joyce a hug. Joyce remembered the woman and called her by name even though it had been years since they last spoke. The woman later explained Joyce had been principal at her daughter's school and Joyce helped them through some tough times.

A few years ago when I re-connected with Joyce's husband Lou after many years, both my wife Debby and I were immediately attracted to Joyce when they visited us at our home in Santa Cruz. They convinced us to take some time and visit Eugene. In the following fall we made a visit and enjoyed their hospitality and a Cal/Oregon football game. We returned the following year for another game—and at that time shopped around and bought a home and made the decision to settle in Oregon. Since moving to Eugene we have had the opportunity on several occasions to spend social time with the Osternig's. A meal at their home was always a joyful fellowship. I always delighted in the lively, spirited conversations we enjoyed during any time we spent with the Osternig's.

When Joyce came to our home for dinner or to watch a football game on the big screen in our media room, she never failed to bring fresh cut flowers from her own garden or a bunch she purchased at the store if the growing season was over. She always paid attention to such thoughtful gestures of friendship and respect for others. As a housewarming gift she gave me a sign that still sits on a shelf in my study. It reads, "OREGON, Where Your Story Begins." It was her way of helping me celebrate that I was now able to continue my career as a writer in this wonderful part of God's world. And, truth be told, she was the inspiration for one of the novels I completed since moving to Eugene.

Joyce Osternig was a classy, unpretentious, down-to-earth woman who thoroughly enjoyed her time with Lou and the many friends they made over the years.

When Joyce was in good health her personality sparkled.

She was never afraid to speak her mind and give an opinion and defend it in lively discussion. She and Lou was a model of a loving relationship between man and woman. They enjoyed each other's companionship and were not afraid to clash with opposing views on numerous political and social issues. That's what made their company such an enjoyable social experience.

Anyone who knew of Joyce's fastidious ways and her playful spirit can appreciate one of my favorite Joyce stories. We were visiting their place a couple of years ago and it was a sunny fall day so she decided to serve dinner on the patio of their lovely back yard. Being accustomed to her elaborate formal dinners, you can imagine the surprise when Joyce invited us to be seated at the table. Then Lou went into the kitchen and brought out a huge pot. He then proceeded to "dump" its contents onto the middle of the table—which was covered with a clean oil-cloth tablecloth. Joyce almost squealed in delight as she saw the surprised look on my face and Debby's face. We were then told it was their special "dump dinner." It was a wonderful collection of corn on the cob, red potatoes, shrimp, and pieces of meat—all we had to do was select and slide a portion to the oil-cloth tablecloth in front of us.

I am one of those people who think of Joyce and Lou as a singular entity—the Osternig's. Now that Joyce is no longer with us physically, I will continue to think of Joyce each time I am in the company of Lou.

I know that Lou and Joyce are Christians who believes in heaven and eternal life after we pass from this world on to the next. I take solace as a Christian in knowing that Joyce is at peace.

I am among those who are saddened and grieve Joyce's passing. I cannot imagine what a profound loss is experienced by Lou as he now continues the Osternig's journey without his mate. But he is accompanied by the memories of so many years of wonderful shared experiences with Joyce that he can keep alive and cherish in the years ahead.

How does one cope with such losses? How does one gather the strength to continue on with life? It is partly through the strength of our religious faith, but it is partly through the support we all give to each other as we continue on with the journey—better off because of Joyce's influence.

Joyce now knows the answer to the great mystery of life.

Those of us who remain behind will continue to struggle with understanding that life for all of us comes to an end.

In celebration of her life and how she was a part of ours, we will recall and retell our special Joyce stories in the years to come.

Thank you, Joyce, for being part of our lives and allowing us to be a part of yours.

* * * * * * * *

Years ago I went through a sensitivity training program designed to get us living folks in the prime of our lives to write our own obituaries. It was a difficult and sobering task—a task I did not feel comfortable doing. Maybe I thought I was tempting fate to pretend I had deceased and to bring my time to some kind of closure.

I have attended and participated in funeral services for many friends and associates and family members over the years. I consider it an honor to find good words to mark and celebrate the passage of people I have known and loved.

I don't like to think about dying. I prefer to think about living. But the older I get the more I want to be prepared to deal with the reality of getting my own house in order.

I want to learn how to feel comfortable talking openly about death as a part of life. I don't want to shy away from it as a taboo topic. I need to feel comfortable saying I am both living and dying. I want to learn to be respectful of these two conditions and allow them to peacefully co-exist in my self-perception.

That's where I think my affiliation with a Christian church helps me put things in perspective. It makes it easier for me to acknowledge the second face I look at in the mirror each morning—the dying face is not the enemy any more than the living face is my friend. They are both real and are partners in my journey—and neither face is on a head that is wearing a black hat!

3

"Be Happy!"

Today is May Day. It is May 1, 2010. May is the fifth month of the year. It is often used as a poetic metaphor to symbolize the early flourishing of life—to "*gather the flowers of May*" meant to enjoy the prime years of life.

It is also an international radiotelephone distress call used by ships and aircraft. Few ships ever radioed the distress signal because they were having a happy day!

Mayday was a serious message. It wasn't about pleasure. It was about pain. A May Day message is different. It is about pleasure and happiness. It is about the celebration of life!

Everyday contains Mayday messages and May Day messages because life and death messages are a part of each day. Our job is to focus on the May Day messages.

As a child we used to celebrate May Day with a ritual of dancing and weaving colorful strips of spring colors around a Maypole. Mothers brought flowers and cookies to our classroom and it was easy to declare the first day of May a "happy day."

Sadly, as years went by and I matured into the bustle of my own career chase, the memory of taking time to celebrate happy days diminished. I grew accustomed to tolerating the rituals and routines surrounding standard seasonal holidays.

What I liked most about May Day celebration was it was just an occasion to dance and party and celebrate life— not any particular holiday that had any significance— like Christmas or Easter, or the Fourth of July. It was just an opportunity to celebrate a happy day.

Why not create a whole bunch of May Day celebrations? In fact, why not create each day a delightful timeout and celebration about a day that makes it a "happy day?"

In dissecting the concept of "a happy day" it occurred to me to question whether an inanimate thing like a day can be described as "happy." When I consulted my dictionary for assistance in the task of understanding the condition of happy and happiness, here's what I found:

Happy—adj. *1. Delighted, pleased, or glad, as over a particular thing. 2. Characterized by or indicative of pleasure, contentment, or joy; a happy mood.* **Happiness** *n. 1. The quality or state of being happy. 2. Good fortune; pleasure; contentment; joy.*

Obviously a day does not feel or exude a mood—the quality of happiness is dependent on human perception.

As I thought further about the concept of happy I realized being happy is not a static condition. Nobody can be said to be a happy person—as though it were a permanent state of being.

Happiness is the opposite of sadness and both are among the hundreds of moods humans can and do experience each day.

Who or what control our tendency to perceive the world around us in a way that puts us in the state of happiness?

Are we supposed to be happy? Is that the normal default condition of the healthy human psyche?

Is the personality characteristic of "happy" a genetic predisposition one inherits from parents, or is the tendency to find pleasure and happiness among the events of our lives an environmentally shaped learned behavior?

What is the role of our religious practice in determining whether we are organized spiritually and theologically to practice a life-style that promotes the personal habit of being happy?

What does the Christian Bible teach followers of Jesus about happy and happiness?

Can it be said that a Christian purposeful life (living for God's will as opposed to living to fulfill our own will) creates and contributes to the molding of a "happy person?"

Does there have to be sadness in the world so we can appreciate the condition of happiness?

In the sadness of a human's funeral, a devout Christian can also perceive happiness in the event because of the belief the dead person is now living an eternal life in a place called Heaven—living in the presence of God, the creator of everything

An agnostic or atheist is unable to find pleasure of happiness in the finality of death.

I have written elsewhere how there are only three things we control in our human life: our beliefs, our perceptions, and our attitudes toward what we perceive and experience. The rest of life is outside our control.

Fundamental to my belief system is the fact there is an all powerful creator of everything who also created Jesus as the son of God through which we Christians find an interpersonal relationship with God the Creator.

Such a belief shapes my perceptions and my attitudes about the events of my life I experience as a mortal human. I believe I am supposed to model my life after the way Jesus lived his life—though I know my human condition prevents me from achieving the sinless life lived by Jesus.

I believe each time I make a decision based on "my will" and not what is in accordance with God's Plan—God's will—I have done something sinful.

I believe because Jesus died in atonement for the sinful nature of humans, my belief in Jesus leads me through my own death into an eternal life in the presence of God the creator of everything.

Why all this focus on God, Jesus, and religion in this book about living and dying in a culture of denial?

Because it is my belief Jesus is the key to living a happy balanced life that pays respect and honor to death's essential and important role.

My faith is based on the greatest, happiest perception one can have about the human condition. It allows me to see in the sadness of death the happiness of eternal life!

A close friend and colleague used to always remind me: "Don't sweat the small stuff; and remember—it's all small stuff!"

Putting things in such perspective, it is easy for me to see I already possess the greatest gift—eternal happiness driven by my faith in the resurrected son of God, Jesus Christ.

All other "small things" which can and do frequently take my attention from the source of greatest happiness and temporarily lead to moments of sadness and unhappiness—all these other things will in fact pass away.

It is the human condition for people to suffer through failing health, broken relationships, lost jobs, financial worries—all are reminders how the human condition is fragile and all humans are headed toward the immutable reality of death as mortals. The richest human will occupy the same "two paces of the vilest earth" as the pauper.

We can, however, choose through our faith, to live a happy life and enjoy the perspective of a generally "happy person" because we believe that through Jesus we enjoy the greatest happiness now and forever.

This personal testimony and philosophy was necessary to state at the beginning of this book because I believe understanding the foundation of my faith is essential to understanding how I am able to practice the habit of confronting the Culture of Denial and allowing the face of my dying self to co-exist with the face of my living self.

I am glad to have discovered the joy that comes from taking the time to focus on confronting the culture of denial and emerging with a balanced perspective and a "Happy Day."

Try it yourself—remember, in God's great plan for humans, we are supposed to be happy—now and in the future!

4

"What Makes A Happy Day?"

Most of us didn't leap from bed this morning jubilant we had awakened to a new day. Many of us began our day chewing on a lot of the left-over stuff still stacked on our plate of worries and concerns from yesterday. Some of us immediately renewed our fears as we stare in the morning mirror and only saw the graying face of a dying self.

I have learned to be more mindful and thankful in starting each day. My first conscious thoughts are gathered in a brief silent prayer. I thank God for awakening me to a new day. It is my way of not taking life for granted. I gather my left-over concerns from yesterday about problems and health challenges faced by my friends and family. I ask God to surround my people with his love and comfort and help them find peace and positive things around with to build their own happy days. Then I get on with bringing my own happy day perspective to the day God has created especially for me!

What does it take to classify a new day as a "happy day?" When the sun is shining it is a happy day. When it is raining it is a happy day. When the tulips and daffodils blossom in our front yard it is a happy day. When the flowers are gone and the trees are barren of leaves, it is a happy day.

Get my point? A happy day isn't defined by what is happening around us. It is defined by how we perceive and react to all the dynamics of life. We define what makes it a happy day. It is that simple.

Then why do so many people go through life so somber and seldom filled with joy? Why do so few people practice the habit of celebrating happy days?

Sadly, many have fallen into the habit of waking up each day with the attitude they must get through the day—hoping "this too shall pass" and tomorrow will be a better day—or, "if I can only get through the week so I can enjoy the weekend."

I realize things happen that frustrate and anger, disappoint, and provide grief to people each day—that's life. I don't advocate people pretend such emotions are not real or don't exist. I don't advocate people retreat into some artificial Pollyanna shell of denial in which one refuses to see how bad things can and do happen to good people.

What I advocate is that people keep their eyes open to the things in each day that can be a source of joy, satisfaction, peace, and comfort.

What are the sources of "happy day" perceptions? That's the challenge for individuals. That's what I undertook to determine as I started using my Happy Day Dollar celebration technique. I wanted to look back over several months of applying such a discipline to see if there were patterns in my perceptions and certain types of things that lent themselves to my own "happy day" perspective.

I do not have a prescribed technique for centering on happy. Instead, all I can do is share with readers what are my "topoi"—my places—where I go to focus on finding sources of peace, contentment, inspiration, and insight.

What makes today a "happy day" for you?

It isn't sufficient to scoff and answer, "*Nothing!*"

If you persist and insist on saying nothing is good about today—then my challenge to you is this: *"Tell me the last time you had a happy day? What made it happy?*

Or, answer me this question, *"What has to happen today to make it a happy day?"*

When you answer such a question, look at who or what was in control of such a thing happening or not happening? How many of your "happy days" are created because things happen that are out of your control? Wouldn't it be a better if you could learn how to define a happy day so you controlled the situation?

If you are someone who thinks the only happy days are "sunny days" then you should move to a sunny part of the world—you know, like Florida or New Orleans. Get my point? Or, did you forget that Katrina visited the sunny states not too long ago?

Don't look for geographic solutions to a life where you can escape from having crappy, unhappy days.

Remember the cartoon character in Little Abner—the poor guy who had the little rain cloud hanging over his head wherever he went? It always rained on his parade wherever he was or whatever he was doing.

If you haven't taken control of your perceptions sufficiently so you can declare each day a "happy day" then you run the risk of living the days of your life under a similar perpetual cloud of gloom.

When my wife and I moved from sunny Monterey Bay in California to Eugene, Oregon, many friends were quick to point out that "it rains all the time in Oregon."

I soon learned rain in Oregon is real—but it is what caused the lush green and golden state of Oregon. I learned, too, that what needs to be said is even though it rains often, there are spectacular clearings between the showers—often several times during an otherwise wet weather day forecast.

It is important for us to develop the perception that allows us to see the blue sky, and the sun that occurs between the rain storms. That's the way I make an otherwise rainy day a "happy day" perception.

5

"Creating A 'Happy Day' Art"

I would never write and sell a book under the title of "The Art of Dying." Over my years I have observed many people coping with the reality of their own death. I do believe there is indeed an "art" to balancing living with dying. I am just not experienced or perceptive enough to fashion the principles of such an art. I certainly am not prepared based on my religious and personal beliefs and values, to undertake such a mission.

If anyone could have written down the principles of the art of dying, however, I did meet one extraordinary woman who would have been up to such a task. Her name was Gloria Lero—Sister Gloria, a member of the Adrian, Michigan Order of Dominican Sisters.

Debby and I marveled as we watched her go about her work as manager of the Dominican Hospital gift shop even though she was living with a terminal, incurable

49

form of cancer. It eventually took her life, but she was someone who cheerfully milked every last bit of fuel from her failing, frail body. She relished life and was not about to let the reality of cancer deny her of the pleasure of a single happy day.

She loved to play golf and it was fitting that with a lot of support from others, a couple of weeks before her death, she was able to travel to the Bishop of Monterey's golf tournament where I had the pleasure of playing in the foursome that proved to be her last round of golf.

I do not underplay the reality she was a devout Catholic sister who practiced the art of Christian living in her daily interactions with all who came in contact with her. She found reasons to smile through the crappy times of her medical treatment. She was never discouraged. She was not sad she was actively dying because she was happy she could still be actively living as well.

In the end she died among the love and support of her sister fellowship—and continued her journey from that final moment.

I regret not having the wisdom and insight to sit down with Sister Gloria and write down everything she could tell me about how it was possible to look at the face of death, smile, and get on with living.

Twelve years ago I did have the audacity to write a book entitled **The Art of Awe.** I suppose at the time I thought that helping people focus on the sources of "awe" would be another tool in their medicine bag that would enable them to transcend any thoughts about death and dying.

The photo on the cover was the puppy face of our ten-week old golden retriever, Luke. He was in a field of grass on the bluffs near our house on the Monterey Bay sniffing the scent of a tiny golden poppy. Today that old dog is still with us and is lying on the cool tile outside my study door as I write these words. He is still one of the things about my days I celebrate often.

The purpose of that earlier book was to inspire readers to look around and discover all the "awe" that surrounded them daily. I even believed it was possible to create what I called "the art of awe" which I defined as follows: "*awe is the art of braiding thoughts with feelings to create a story about a moment in time which validates our belief in God Grand Scheme of Things.*"

I went on to explain that "*The first principle of the art of awe is that awe does not reside in the external experience. Awe is not in the spectacular sunset; awe is in the eye of the beholder. We must necessarily be a function of how we think, feel, and believe about events. The topoi (places) of awe dwell within us.*

Then in the conclusion of that book's preface, I explained:

"*Our challenge is to see the extraordinary in the ordinary. Awe validates for us that there is a God's Grand Scheme of Things. It helps us see the connection between the seemingly isolated experiences of a human*

*day and an awesome, all-purposeful grand design. Awe
allows us to celebrate that we do fit into the design, that
we are a part. And, most wonderful of all, we have the
capacity to know and feel how our existence is part of
God's design.*

I had to chuckle to realize I am still dogged in my pursuit
of championing a positive, optimistic perspective on life.
Now I am able to do it while acknowledging the
important positive role death plays in the process.

In fact, I was somewhat taken back when I re-read an
introductory quote to chapter 8 of that book, "A Day in
the *Awe* of the Beholder." It was a poem by an unknown
author. It read:

*Normal day
Let me learn from you,
Savor you,
Bless you,
Before we depart.
Let me not pass you by in quest of some rare and perfect
tomorrow.*

Wow! Here I am, twelve years later, coping with the
reality of grieving a friend's death and once again
turning to my past interest in finding the moments of
awe, the stuff from which we craft happy days.

In this process of grieving, I realize my Christian values
have matured. I now have a clearer vision of what I was

trying to say when I was describing what I then called "the art of awe."

Today I am calling it the art of "centering on happy." Like in my earlier endeavor I have a constructed another list of principles that appear to be involved understanding how to transform ordinary days into happy days.

First Principle: God is the creator of all our DAYS. All of God's days are good days, but it is up to us to perceive them as Happy Days.

Second Principle: God gave us our five human senses so we could perceive things around us and be in control of three things: our beliefs, our attitudes, and our perceptions. Everything else is outside our control.

Third Principle: Even though God is the author of all our days, we humans are the creator of HAPPY DAYS. Such days are the product of human perceptions—likewise, so are Crappy Days. Such perceptions become our daily reality.

Fourth Principle: When we can find happiness in death because of our belief in eternal life beyond our mortality, we have the belief basis for finding happiness in any of the fleeting hardships we might confront in any day of our life. Regardless of the cross of suffering we might bear in any day of our life, we realize "this too shall pass." A strong belief in an eternal life gives us the ultimate and unwavering happy day perspective!

Fifth Principle: Most often it is not what we accomplish, but what we experience that is the greatest source from which we construct a happy day perspective. A book, a walk, a friendship, a recollection made in a quiet moment of contemplation, can often be an experience worth holding up and giving thanks to God for enabling as the material of our happy day perception. God wants us to experience the awesomeness of his great creation, despite any of the hardships that fall upon us during our personal journey. God wants our life experience to be a good experience. That's why God gave us the great commission to be in charge of our beliefs, attitudes, and perceptions.

* * * * * * * *

Sister Gloria was probably quite familiar with these principles. They were ingrained into her healthy outlook on life. She was indeed blessed with the remarkable perception that allowed her to practice the art of the happy day in how she lived her life.

Today I will make a contribution to our Happy Dollar container in honor of Gloria. Recalling memories of her enriched my day and made it a happy day.

6

"Mingling the Past with the Present"

I have finally learned not to discard past memories—happy and crappy—like yesterday's newspapers. Like my recollection of Sister Gloria, memories have a role in helping us shape our current happy day perspective.

The longer we live the more memories we have to co-mingle with perceptions of things happening in the present time. Many a new happy day can be constructed from creating the metaphor of understanding that comes from seeing the present in relationship to the past.

Our memories of past times when death took a family and friend can also help us today develop a balanced approach to living and dying each day.

In preparing my thoughts to write about death, I rummaged through my memory to my earliest recollections of people around me dying. My first recollection was the death of "Cookie" the jovial, rotund black woman who worked at my father's company and frequently baby-sat my sister and me when we were five and six years old living in San Francisco.

I remember a lot of people gathered at our home one day after her funeral. My sister and I were told Cookie had died. We struggled to understand what it meant to die. My folks explained that we would never see Cookie again—but that she had gone to heaven to be with God.

Later that evening I remember getting a panicky feeling and anxiously asking my father if everybody had to die—even if they were good? He told me "yes." I cried and hugged him and said I didn't want him to die. He embraced me back and kissed me on my forehead and promised he wouldn't die for a long time—not until I was all grown up. I trusted everything my father said so with that matter settled, I stopped worrying about dying.

Death became real to me several years later when my childhood friend Joe Pellizari died with a form of leukemia. He wasn't an old person or a grown up. He was a kid. That's when I realized death could happen to me at any time. For several weeks I worried about dying. Fortunately, all the activities of summer helped erase my fears. I was totally absorbed in living and fully re-absorbed into the culture of denial. Death was still a condition that happened to everybody else and to members of their family—not mine.

When my father died of a sudden-death heart attack at age 51 I was stunned. I had just started my own adult life after graduating from college and heading off with a new bride to graduate school at the University of Oregon. I was angry and it just didn't seem fair. His funeral was a time of denial and not closure for me. I was almost desperate to have a son so I could replace the life that was taken from our family through dad's untimely death. A little over a year later my oldest son Timothy was born. The joy of that birth seemed to somehow checkmate the cruel move made by death.

For much of my adult life I had the lingering sense in the back of my mind that I was going to die at age 51—just like my dad. When that time came and passed I felt like I was living on borrowed time.

Several other folks in my family have since passed in death and I have lived more than a decade and a half longer than my father. I have seen several people—including my mother—linger in old age and wither away in a nursing home—barely cognizant of the world around them or who they were. In the end, my mother barely recognized me when I visited.

Now I am a senior member of my own family tree—the oldest male in the Hite clan. I relish there are grandsons who will carry forward my family name. I think I am beginning to settle into the patriarch role with dignity.

Now, instead of worrying when death will arrive, I am learning to face the reality and to move on with living and creating happy days by co-mingling the past with the present. Maybe I am finally learning to truly practice the art of awe in my everyday life. Maybe it is really just another name for "the art of dying?

I was reminded of this strange alchemy of past and present when I recently attended the annual University of Oregon Twilight Track meet at the venerable Hayward Field. It was for me one of those places of awe I wrote about decades ago.

Let me explain what happened.

My friend Lou is a professor-emeritus at the university. His professional relationship with the athletic department through his teaching and research in the field of exercise physiology and sports medicine earned him an invitation to view the meet from the balcony of the Bowerman Building that stands overlooking the starting line for sprints on the west side of the stadium. I was invited as his guest. Ordinarily we would have used my season-tickets and enjoyed the perspective five rows up in the stands from the finish line. The balcony was a superior venue—as was the accompanying fellowship of the other guests.

In addition to the physical education faculty and their guests, the event was attended by many old-timers who had various connections with the university sport's department over the past several decades.

The common thread running through the social conversation was how most of these senior citizens were former athletes themselves—and most were still impassion to continue with their various running, skiing, hiking and physical activities.

I was surprised however, how many didn't hesitate to volunteer in the course of conversations how they were plagued with hip or knee problems and a variety of aches and pains associated with the reality that their athletic body was breaking down through the normal aging process. Many had knee and hip replacements—or arthroscopic surgery to repair tears and ruptures.

As we stood along the railing looking down at the physically fit Oregon track athletes gathering outside the locker room and awaiting their opportunity to show their stuff, it struck me how I was participating in the "now" of the moment from an entirely different perspective.

If I hadn't been a student athlete I couldn't appreciate the efforts each person on the track below was making in the pursuit of their own potential.

The now of the moment was enhanced by the contrast between the youth below and the aching, aging bodies of the older folks on the balcony above! We were their future; they were our past. Both were important in creating my awesome perception of the "now" of the moment!

Those of us on the balcony traded stories about past recollections of Oregon track greatness—great races we had seen on the track in the years past.

As the meet progressed and threatening rain clouds began to fill the evening sky, I savored all the experiences of the moment. I relished the privilege of talking with Vin Lannana, the track coach who returned the Oregon program to the greatness of the Bowerman years. I felt honored to be among the old-timers on the balcony. I relished the reality I was not alone in dealing with my aches and pains as my aging once athletic body continues to lose it resilience.

I didn't long to return to the youthful years represented by the aspirations and dreams of the young athletes on the field below. I'd been there, done that, though not to the level of excellent level of achievement of most of the gifted Oregon athletes down below. It was now their time to shine. But I could still be a part of the excitement of the evening as it unfolded.

I cheered with the same passion and enthusiasm for the Oregon sophomore Matt Centrowicz's first sub-four minute mile as I did when Steve Prefontaine accomplished the same feat forty-years ago.

After the meet as Lou and I walked across campus in the chilly evening air I savored flashback memories of my brief-five years as a graduate student crossing campus and heading to the library or my office to work on my dissertation.

We cannot separate the "now" of the moment from the vast storehouse of past memories. Indeed, the memories enrich the fullness of now experiences.

When I finally got home I didn't hesitate to call Debby at her mom's home in Paradise, CA where she was visiting to celebrate Mother's Day. Debby knew from the excitement in my voice it had been an awesome evening. When I finished my report about all the fantastic performances, Debby laughed.

"I don't have to guess what you're going to celebrate with a happy dollar tonight when you go upstairs to bed."

She was right. I stuffed several bills into our container. It wasn't so much the performance of the athletes at the meet that made me celebrate that day as a "happy day." It was what the track meet brought together and taught me about how awesome happy days can be created when we co-mingle the past with the present.

I learned how past memories spice and flavor how we live in the "now" of a current happy day.

7

"Beyond Productivity"

At a recent Rotary meeting I listened carefully as fellow Rotarians stood up and made Happy Dollar declarations and added their dollars to our weekly club fundraising collection.

A young attorney celebrated that he and his partner settled a pending litigation out of court. Another person talked about getting his business better organized. Another person talked about a promotion she had received in her role at the university. The speaker that evening was the President of Oregon State University and he did a first rate job of enumerating all the accomplishments of the university and his vision for an even more productive future.

As I listened I realized since retiring from my hospital administrator role, the concept of measuring worth in terms of productivity seemed less important to how I viewed what made my days happy. The business of business, however, was a central theme in fashioning club members' perception of their happy days.

As was the normal case, people celebrated events, accomplishments, and things that happened recently they deemed worthy of a boast. The proclamations confirmed for me how we grab hold of the tangible things we produce in our lives and use such things to construct our perception of a happy day. My challenge to readers is to move beyond this business cult that worships productivity.

Whether we like it or not we are a "productivity-driven" society in which the volume of work completed is the measure of success. We ask ourselves, "How much work did we get done today?" We measure worth in terms of "What do you do?"

It is time for us to ask the question of one's social value differently if we want to learn the art of relishing life a day at a time. Perhaps the better phrased question is, "What did you experience today?"

Perhaps we need to give ourselves permission to value and celebrate "heightened awareness" as a noteworthy experience worthy of warranting a happy day celebration.

One way to accomplish this is to move beyond the tendency to focus attention on the perceived and pay attention to the perceivers. We seldom give much thought to the everyday presence of the faculties through which we perceive all that comprises a happy day.

I am referring, of course to the perceivers—the senses we use to construct our symphony of everyday awareness. Let's give credit where credit is due. If it were not for our sense of sight, sound, touch, taste and smell, there would be little way of getting in tune with the world around us.

I have yet to hear anyone proclaim they are contributing a happy dollar to the evening's fundraising effort because they are happy they have been able to see things through their eye-sight. I have not heard any happy dollar testimonials celebrating the faculty of hearing.

Isn't it curious how we take for granted these awesome senses and move ever so quickly to the so-called more important things in life?

It is only when one or more of these instruments get out of tune with the other perceiver faculties and fail us in receiving clear messages that we realize how much happiness each contribute to our daily living experience.

Recently a close friend of mine was infected with something that caused his lower limbs to lose a good portion of their sensory awareness—meaning a sense of numbness created noise in his normally healthy central nervous system.

I know that in all the years I have known him, he never said to me how happy he was on a given day because of how well his central nervous system allowed him to relate to the everyday tasks of moving through his life's journey.

Hopefully when the condition subsides and he returns to a more normal condition of sensory awareness in his lower extremities, he will no longer take for granted this incredible part of the instruments through which we create the symphony of life around us.

I though how ironic it is that as we age and our healthy body gives way to various aging processes, we stop being so focused on what we achieve—as many of us are retired and our professional careers are behind us. Instead, we become focused on how we are losing our finely tuned faculties. We become hard of hearing; our eye-sight fails; our sense of taste diminishes; our sense of smell weakens. I am reminded of Shakespeare's famous "ages of man" soliloquy, "sans eyes, sans hair, sans teeth, sans everything."

What will it take in our lives to cause us to proclaim a happy day because we are still fully equipped to sense all the sights, sounds, tastes, smells, and textures of substances we encounter in a day's journey?

Perhaps it is human nature to take for granted these faculties until we notice we are losing one or more. Sadly, for many of us, these gifts are not valued as long as they are working well—but they become priceless when they no longer work.

Why not single out one faculty on a regular basis and construct a happy day perception not on what is perceived but on being thankful for the faculty through which it is perceived.

How can we celebrate and create a happy day perception that focuses on hearing? Suppose we listen and make a list of the things we heard in our everyday surroundings that we were not conscious of in our normal routine. Celebrate hearing the sound of a distant train whistle in the middle of the night. Celebrate listening to the rustling of leaves as the wind blows through the branches. Celebrate listen to the variety of bird sounds one can hear in the back yard as various birds come and go to the bird-feeders.

How can we become more attuned to the symphony of sights and sounds and smells that co-mingle and create the world around us—how can we heighten our awareness of the container and not the contained accomplishments that ordinarily mark the boundaries of a happy day?

How much of the experience of a day have we learned to block out of awareness as we focus on an activity or achievement we want to accomplish. Do we mow the lawn and not note the smell of the fresh cut grass as we empty the grass-catcher into the yard-waste container? Do we run around the track and focus our daily training on the surface of the track or do we look up at the cloud formations, smell the flower scents in the air, the fresh cut grass in the nearby field, and hear the stream of background city sounds that fill the air?

What happens when our senses do begin to diminish and our sensory faculties begin to fail us? How can such a condition contribute to a "happy day" perception?

We learn to compensate—like the blind person who has incredible acute senses of hearing and touch.

When we can't run as far or as fast, or even walk as far as we used to do in a daily routine, we can use assistive devices to get to where we want to be—but even greater, when we arrive, we can heighten our awareness of the sights and sounds of that new surroundings.

Many of us spend a lifetime focused on work productivity. It is hard to step away from the work-performance standard of success and start looking at a happy day success in terms of what we experience, not what we produced.

I remember from my college philosophy class the famous proclamation of Rene Descartes made about life, "I think, therefore I am." I am more inclined to expand the concept to declare, "I sense with all my God given-senses the experiences contained in a happy day—therefore I am a healthy child of God."

A healthy child of God learns to celebrate the experience of life as well or more so than the accomplishments of life.

8

"God Produces and we Perceive"

I recently listened to a popular television evangelist exhort his large arena audience to understand how all blessings and opportunities are created and produced by God. When we receive a promotion, accomplish a major achievement, or receive a contract we didn't expect to land, it is not something we should use to elevate our own ego or self-esteem. The evangelist's message was clear: the larger God elevates your success, the smaller and more humble you should be in receiving the gift.

Regardless of the magnitude of what we celebrate about the happy day things we perceive, we need to be humble and give credit and honor to God the creator of everything. It is God who enables us to achieve. It is also God who enables us to perceive. The more we prosper and enjoy the blessings of our own happy days, the more we need to give glory and honor to God.

I just took a walk around a one-mile loop of the neighborhood where we live here in Eugene and thought about that evangelist's message. Today is a chilly, overcast grey day that does not invite folks out to work in their yards and gardens. It a day that those cooped up inside an office building will not notice as anything special or something they long to enjoy as an alternative to their office space.

Ordinarily, I put on my running shoes and sweats and jog through the loop. This afternoon, however, I decided not to be productive and check "workout" off of my to-do list. I wanted to see if it was different when viewed from the eyes of a walker.

I found out it is different. I never noticed the glorious wrap of pinkish-white dogwood blossoms on the tree at the end corner where I normally turn left and head down Carthage toward River Road. I also noticed the vivid colors of all the flowers in the yards along Carthage—and how well groomed each yard is along the street. Ordinarily, my eyes are focused on the pavement in front of me as I carefully stride through my workout.

I enjoyed not being productive but instead just being perceptive and seeing things for the first time. I smiled and greeted three different people out walking their dogs—normally, I don't make eye contact and pretend like I am totally focused on my running.

I am highly skilled at tuning things out of my everyday awareness so I can focus on accomplishing something I think is important. I can sit for hours in front of my computer and exercise the discipline of being a creative writer.

It is a curious thing, however, that once I finish a writing project and receive the final hard-copy of my latest book, there is a discomfort in me. I seem dissatisfied with the accomplishment and anxious to get on with the next book.

I wonder if that is a carry-over from a work culture where one can never rest their laurels on what was accomplished in the past. It is always necessary to respond to "what are you going to do for me today!"

The same mentality seems to drive many people when they begin to accumulate wealth. How much is enough? When does one stop worrying about producing wealth and focus on enjoying the experience one can have in life after the basics of food and shelter are funded?

The wealth we accumulate as a result of being productive in our work behavior is not our wealth. We hold it in trust for God who created and produced the opportunities that enables us to acquire the wealth. If we use that wealth only for our selfish purposes and don't find ways to share the surplus, then we are not creating the kind of health, happy days God intended us to enjoy.

I am constantly reminded in my retirement that I enjoy an income that is no longer tied to my work productivity. I have paid off all my debts and have no outstanding credit debt or mortgages. I now open up my pocket to more contributions to charitable, not-for-profit causes than I ever did while I was working. Why? I now realize that God has taken care of all my needs for all these years and God has put me in a comfortable position in my retirement years to where I don't have to worry about money.

What I do give concern to is making sure I use what I call my "tithing" dollars to help others.

Part of what makes a happy day for me these days is realizing I am a servant of God in the way I distribute my limited philanthropy to serve the needs of my community.

God has always been the source of my productivity and my achievements even though I seldom gave God the credit. Now I am determined to relish the happy day experience of life and not just the accumulation of material trophies and things.

9

"Celebrating Variety"

Wednesday, May 12, 3010. According to my daily journal I affectionately call **Grandpa's Time Machine**, this day is my 830th day of our move to Oregon. It is also my 1723rd day since I took off my necktie and retired from my thirty-year career as a hospital administrator.

As an addicted daily journalist, I became aware of how much we pattern our lives through the rituals of everyday activities dictated by work routines and general social obligations created by the need to celebrate holidays and special events like birthdays and anniversaries.

Toward the end of my work career I used to jokingly refer to these personal and professional patterns of predictable behavior as my "Groundhog Day" prison. The metaphor was borrowed from the classic Bill Murray film of the same name. In the film Murray awakens time and time again into the same day—his coverage of the celebrated holiday where the community looks to see if the groundhog sees his shadow and whether there will be six more weeks of winter.

I was not surprised to see in my journal record a very predictable patterns of events—with only a few day time variation, it appeared I was dealing with the same things years after year—board retreats, vacations, holidays, special events, etc. My yearly patterns were remarkable predictable. I vowed when I retired that I would break out of such an established pattern and enjoy the refreshing newness of a new life in a new community. That was one of the prime reasons I relished the move Debby and I made to Oregon. I was convinced it would be key to an absolute escape from the Groundhog Day existence I crafted in my professional career.

Guess what? It isn't that easy to change. I can already see the tendency to create a new pattern of structure and ritual and routine during my year since I retired 1723 days ago!

Debby is at her mother's place in Paradise. That's where she has been for the past five years during this Mother's Day holiday period. I've also started new patterns. I go on Tuesdays evenings to Rotary. I go on Sundays to church with Debby. I am in my study writing from 9:30 to 3:30 and then break and head to the nearby middle-school all-weather track for a two-mile workout. And, I am in the routine of attending the annual sporting events here in Eugene like the University of Oregon Twilight Track meet with my friend Lou.

I realize patterns are inescapable and not necessarily undesirable. We are, after all, structuring, organizing creatures. We develop habits and routines—they help us navigate through the thousand of distractions that can keep us from focusing on the things we believe are important to experience and accomplish during our journey.

Occasionally, however, it is good to step back and celebrate the creation of a happy day that is purposefully and deliberately disruptive of normal routines. I was determined to do that this morning as I awakened to the day.

Instead of getting showered, shaved, dressed, and going down to my yogurt and granola breakfast and then heading to my study to begin my morning's work as a writer, I altered the routine.

I still fed the ducks on our pond with their daily allotment of cracked corn—as per the instruction Debby left before departing on her visit to her mom's. I also fed the cat and brought in the morning newspaper. That's where I abandoned the routine.

I climbed into my car and drove seven miles down to one of the favorite places Debby and I occasionally go after church for a Sunday breakfast—the Original Pancake House. It is an establishment owned by a couple Debby met in the church group she accompanied on a recent tour of Israel to visit the Christian holy places.

After enjoying some bacon and eggs and reading the morning newspaper at a table for one in the back of the restaurant, I returned to my car and drove to a nearby Border's Book Store. There I browsed and shopped for some new books. I realized how long it had been since I allowed myself the pleasure of cruising through tables of new fiction and non-fiction books and relishing the variety of thoughts and ideas expressed in books.

When I finally drove into my garage back home it was almost noon. Under normal circumstances I would have spent the morning in front of my computer. My little diversion had been an enjoyable alternative to my routine.

It certainly wasn't an earth-shaking alteration in my current life-style to break away from my routine—but it was important for me to realize and be conscious of patterns. If we are not careful, they can become insidious and stifling. Patterns and routines can steal from us the passion to continually explore new possibilities in how we live our happy days.

I cherish the time I now have made available to focus my days on my passion for writing. I realize, though, that like everything else in life, I need to resist becoming singular in my focus. If I don't, then I am still a victim of not being in control of how I spend the precious currency of my life's remaining time.

The lesson I learned is the one I will celebrate tonight when I stuff some happy dollars into the container that sits atop our bedroom dresser. I made my day happier because I playfully chose to break routine and alter my familiar way of structuring my day.

10

"When I write, I write"

Today I celebrate as the focus of my happy day dollar the joy I have because I am a writer. And, what better way to celebrate than tell a story.

I noted in my daily journal entry for this day in May 2003 how I was part of our senior management team's quarterly training seminar for Dominican Hospital's full management team. We took a great deal of pride in creating and teaching the curriculum ourselves instead of bringing in outside experts.

The seminars took place at a lovely little conference center nestled in the foothills of the Santa Cruz mountains. It was appropriately called Happy Valley and had the reputation for serving awesome fresh-made "sticky-buns" and other pastries that gave a sugar jolt to morning coffee drinkers and an aroma that lingered in the adjacent conference room for much of the day.

It was an easy fifteen-minute drive from the hospital but was far enough away so participants didn't feel compelled to be constantly checking in on their department activities.

We frequently built our management training around themes that related to how best to improve the operational quality of the hospital and improve the quality of clinical care.

On this particular day, we used a wonderfully inspirational film that featured Dewitt Jones, a former National Geographic photographer who told his story about travelling the world to capture on film the theme of "what's right in the world."

My favorite part of the video focused on a series of photos he took of a Scottish woman weaver. He asked her what she thought about when she was weaving, to which she replied, "Whether I am going to run out of thread!" Then immediately after she responded, as if she sensed Dewitt was disappointed with her response, she added, "When I weave, I weave."

Her message was clear—when you are really into something—it is all consuming—it becomes your very being. Dewitt concluded his interview by explaining how the woman wanted to be the best weaver she could be—not the best IN the world, but the best FOR the world!

In that same film I realized that Dewitt's experience as a photographer taught him that what we believe is more important that what we see—a curious conclusion from a man who made his living seeking to find the perfect picture—the picture that caught the essence of its subject.

He proclaimed that if we believe, then we will learn to see. It was his way of saying that perceiving is a function of believing.

Many of the concepts we taught in those management seminars still resonate with me today—especially the wisdom of people like Dewitt Jones.

I realize that if he were to ask me what I think about when I am engrossed in my daily writing activity I would be inclined to answer as the old Scottish weaver answered—"when I write, I write." It is an all consuming activity that focuses my mind on bringing concepts and ideas into word that can capture on the page the images and thoughts that dance around in my imagination.

It doesn't make any difference whether I am writing fiction or non-fiction. When I write I listen to the voice inside my head that through some mysterious alchemy God stirred into my being speaks to me.

I know I am supposed to be a writer. Why do I hold such a strong belief? Because when a day passes I don't write I feel less than satisfied. When I write I feel happy and fulfilled—like I am doing what I God gifted me to do.

I have yet to write anything that has gotten me acclaim as a writer. Perhaps that is a blessing in disguise. I am enjoying God's gift and I alone appreciate it is God's gift. If and when any of my writing becomes noteworthy in the larger world, then I need to be humble and realize that it is best FOR the world because it is God's gift, not mine.

When each of us creates our happy day celebrations, each of us has a special gift. Each of us can proclaim "when I BLANK, I BLANK."

Whatever your gift you name and use to fill in the blank, I hope you frequently take time to realize it is God's gift designed to allow you to be the best FOR the world.

11

"Books Transform"

Emily Dickinson provided me with one of my best metaphors for viewing the face of death in my everyday life.

In her poetic mind's eye, she perceived death as a gentleman's caller who realized she was so busy living that she didn't have time to get prepared and worry about the arrival of death. I think Emily Dickinson would have gotten along quite nicely with my friend Sister Gloria who I wrote about several chapters ago.

Her most famous poem "Because I could not stop for death, he kindly stopped for me," says it best for me. Death is a friend and not a foe, but he has to catch up with us because we don't dally around dragging our feet waiting for the gentleman caller to stop by for us.

Today I decided to dedicate my happy day perspective to my recollections of the writings of Emily Dickinson. I was especially thoughtful about her imagery in another one of her classic poems, "There Is No Frigate Like a Book."

The reclusive spinster seldom traveled far from her Boston home in a physical sense. Indeed, there are stories about how she lowered messages in a basket from her second story bedroom down to people at the street level instead of descending the stairs for an interpersonal interaction.

Her poetic imagery captured for me the awesome power of a book to transform a day into an adventure in some exotic far away land. Books also introduce us into the inner workings of great thinkers who struggled to fashion their unique perspective on how the world around us works.

One of the books I bought recently during my junket to Border's Books bore the eye catching title THE LANGUAGE GOD TALKS—subtitle, On Science and Religion. When I saw the author's name I hastily purchased passage on his frigate because I wanted to know how Herman Wouk, the esteemed Pulitzer Prize novelist of The Cain Mutiny, thought about God and science.

I wasn't disappointed. The book took me on a fascinating voyage through recent scientific history and the writing career of Wouk. It ended as it began with curious encounters with the famous nuclear physicist Nobel Prize winner Richard Fenyman.

The book's title was the metaphor fashioned by the Nobel scientist and the Pulitzer writer when the two met at Cal Tech for an interview Wouk wanted to conduct with the scientist.

According to Wouk the scientist asked him, "Do you know calculus?" to which Wouk replied "No."

The scientist admonished him, "You had better learn it. It is the language God talks."

In the fantastic journey through Wouk's perceptions of many of the great scientific discovers of the past century, he reflects his dogged adherence to his orthodox Jewish belief system—continually referring back to studying the Talmud under the tutelage of his grandfather. Wouk looked to the wisdom of the scriptures and not the calculus of science for his answers about the nature of the universe and man's role on this stage.

He recognizes, though, that Fenyman's scientific view was agnostic at its core, evidenced by this quote:

"It doesn't seem to me that this fantastically marvelous universe, this tremendous range of time and space and different kinds of animals, and all the different planets, and all these atoms with all their motions, and so on, all this complicated thing can merely be a stage so that God can watch human beings struggle for good and evil—

which is the view that religion has. The stage is too big for the drama."

Undaunted by such a challenge, Wouk respectfully disagrees with his esteemed acquaintance and continues searching for ways to balance religion and God—but confessing all along he relies on non-science because he has not mastered what Fenyman calls "the language of God"—calculus.

I was struck by one particular quote from another Nobel scientist, Steven Weinberg—a thinker attributed with fashioning the big bang theory of creation and expressed in landmark book, The First Three Minutes. Wouk describes the agnostic picture Weinberg paints in that book:

"The more the universe seems comprehensible the more it also seems pointless. . . .The effort to understand the universe is one of the very few things that lifts human life a little about the level of farce, and give it some of the grace of tragedy."

Wouk notes other insights from Weinberg that provides a glimmer of hope for scientists who see the universe as devoid of any creator. Weinberg concludes:

"One of the great achievements of science has been, if not to make it impossible for intelligent people to be religious, then at least to make it possible for them not to be religious. We should not retreat from this accomplishment."

When I finally disembarked from Wouk's frigate, I was in awe of how deftly the humanist Wouk used his great talents as a writer to make his case for God the creator of everything. He helped me reinforce my own beliefs as I struggle with how to merge my scientific understanding of the universe with my religious views as a Christian.

Without denying readers the joy of their own discovery, I will not speak to how Wouk achieves his mission—but he does, and he does so by drawing on excerpts from his own fictional works.

I encourage readers to book passage on Wouk's fascinating frigate as it overviews the awesome landmark scientific achievements in understanding the vastness of our modern perspective of the universe.

It took me the better part of this day to digest Wouk little book. When I closed the cover and arrived back into the reality of the surroundings of my front room I realized Dickinson was right, "There is no frigate like a book" to transform what could have been a self-centered otherwise mundane and perhaps even crappy day into a happy day for me!

Thank you for the happy day, Herman Wouk—and thank you God for creating such a man as part of your awesome plan!

12

"A Crappy Day"

A crappy experience may well be necessary so we can fully appreciate a happy experience—just like the presence of the dying face of death makes us appreciate all the more the living face. Our challenge is to appreciate the two opposites and blend them into the balance perspective of a happy day. Each validates the importance of the other.

What would it be like if we didn't have our senses to perceive all the stuff God created and surrounded us with?

We get a clue every night when we fall asleep. Even though our mind may be active with images and dreams conjured from our library collection of memories, we do remove ourselves from the conscious task of perceiving with our senses.

For some of us, even when we awake and start through our daily activities, we put many of our sensory equipment on half-power. In effect, we learn how to not perceive most of what is happening around us. Why? Because we only want to attend to the stuff we think is important in maintaining our well-being.

Each of us take control of our sight, sound, touch, smell and taste and calibrate these preceptors to detect and monitor only the things we need to sense so we can be successful in living the kind of life we fashion for ourselves.

In the evening when we walk our old Golden Retriever through the neighborhood there are certain spots where Luke pauses to sniff and then after a few moments, he raises his leg and leaves his own mark.

I jokingly refer to such communication as his "p-mail" stop. I have been told dogs can distinguish hundreds of times more nuisances of smells than humans. I like to think the smell in each dog's urine is not only a unique signature, but somehow animals can and do leave other messages encoded in the smell they leave in their p-mail.

Most of the time I set my sense of smell to alert me to the extremes of pleasure and danger. I have catalogued the smells of my favorite foods cooking in the kitchen. But, truth be known, I don't eat a lot of variety in my food. I do react, however, when I smell the Cinnamon aroma of the gooey-pastry when we walk through the shopping mall. Curiously, I enjoy the smell a lot more than actually purchasing and consuming one of the sugary rolls.

I have a check list of smells that set off my danger alarms—smoke, the smell of gas, the sound of rushing water, or the obnoxious smells of manure or air-pollution from a paper-mill factory.

When I travel to an area where the air is constantly tainted with an obnoxious factory smell—or travel to a coastal mud-flat area where there is an unpleasant smell of the fishy ocean and the bacteria baked wet mud—it doesn't surprise me how locals no longer are aware of the smell. They have learned to live with it and to mask it from their awareness. I suppose those who depend upon the smell-polluting factory or fishy-smell environment can actually respond positively to the odor—knowing that its presence is assurance there will be work and a bright economic future.

The same phenomena of selective perception can plague our other sensors as well. My sense of taste isn't terribly sophisticated—perhaps because I view food as fuel—and, I also have allergies to a variety of spicy seasonings.

We see what we need to see—Eskimo who depend on knowledge about the weather conditions have developed a greater sensitivity to the nature of snow. They distinguish at least six-types of snow where I would simply see snow!

I used to marvel how I could get in my car and head for work along seven miles of surface roads to my office. Many a morning I almost startled myself into the realization I had just driven those seven miles while on sensory auto-pilot. When I stepped out of my car in the parking lot of the hospital where I worked, I could not tell you about anything I'd just done. I couldn't tell you how many stop light I'd stopped at. I couldn't tell you anything about the roadwork being done alongside the road.

I often wondered how much of that sensory auto-pilot was operating on how I went through the rest of my workday. I knew there was a lot more going on around me than what I was perceiving—or needed to perceive in order to accomplish my work mission.

The older I get the more I have allowed myself to become a victim of my own sensory data calibrations. I see what I want and need to see—not everything that is there to see. I hear what I want to hear—not all the distinct sounds being made. In sum, I calibrate my senses so I can make my life more predictable and presumably more controllable.

If you had a crappy day, you might as well have stayed in bed asleep. In fact, truth be told, your crappy day was precisely because you were asleep!

I have written elsewhere that humans are by nature variety reducing, redundancy producing creatures. Just as Nature abhors a vacuum, humans seem to abhor entropy, the tendency toward randomness and unpredictability.

The truth of the matter is we need a healthy balance in the entropy-redundancy equation we use to appreciate each day we live.

Too tight of control of our senses may lead us into the comfortable patterns of our daily rituals and routines, but they can also lay down the redundancy that can set the stage for perceiving crappy days.

Our challenge is to use our senses to heighten our awareness of something new and undetected in our everyday patterns. That's what can often allow us to transform an ordinary or even crappy day, into a happy day.

This is now the proper place to officially define a "**crappy day!**"

A **crappy day** is one that is totally predictable, there are no surprises or "aha" moments of insight. You didn't have to get out of bed to demonstrate it was going to happen. In fact, you actually had all your senses on auto-pilot and calibrated so they perceived exactly the things you wanted them to perceive.

Guess what?

Crappy days are what we do to ourselves, not what somebody else does to us. If you don't want a crappy day, then don't calibrate your preceptors so they produce one.

Happy days require more effort, but it well worth it!

13

"A Happy Mother's Day"

Most of us older adults have already come to terms with—or are coming to terms with—the reality that if things take the normal course we will all be faced with having to bury our mother. I've already buried my mom. Debby's mom is nearing the end of her human journey as well.

Such knowledge is like the ever present other face we see each morning in the mirror—the one we'd like to deny exists. The purpose of such knowledge about the nature of things is to awaken us to the opportunity we have to celebrate the current presence of our mothers who are with us today.

* * * * * * *

Sunday May 8, 2010 was Mother's Day. Almost by definition such traditional holidays beg each of us to make sure the day is fashioned into a "happy day." Who knows how many more days we will be blessed with in which to enjoy the presence of the person through whom God gave us the life we enjoy as humans.

One of the functions of a holiday is to focus our attention on some aspect of life worth a formal celebration. What greater day to celebrate than the one that honors mothers.

When I was doing my daily run through our neighborhood a few minutes ago, I passed by several people working to de-thatch the front lawn of a place around the block from my home. I heard one older woman say to the other, "I got some great flowers from my son and another bunch from my daughter."

The other woman replied, "I got a wonderful card from my daughter. It was the sweetest thing."

I smiled as I passed by and heard the conversation. It was nice to see children took time from their own families and routines to make contact with the person they called "mom."

My wife Debby never had any children from her previous marriage or our marriage. But that doesn't keep us from celebrating mother's day and making it a "happy day" for us as well as the mother we honor—which is this case is Verla—Deb's 87 year- old mother who lives in Paradise, CA.

In the twenty-years I have been married to Debby, I can only recall a couple of years where Debby was unable to arrange her schedule so she could be present at her mom's place to celebrate Mothers' Day.

Debby is with her mom today and I know she is making it a happy day worth celebrating. She left on the trip to Paradise a few days ago fully equipped to refurbish the deck of her mom's house and freshen-up the surface of the deck with a new all-weather astro-turf cover.

Accompanying Debby on the 400 mile car trip was our 12 year-old golden retriever, Luke. He is Deb's child in every sense of the word. He is, unfortunately, in failing health, and we are enjoying his remaining days a day at a time. His presence with her will make it a happy Mothers' Day for Debby.

Deb and her mom will go to church, work in the yard, and then spend time with Deb's younger sister and her family who also live in Paradise. They will all have a dinner and celebrate Verla's continuing health and vital presence in their lives.

By contrast, my mother passed on to a better place over a decade ago. I was not as close to my mom as Debby is to Verla—but I never failed to do things to honor my mother on this special day.

Now on Mothers' Day I take time to reflect and resurrect memories of the past good-times my mother fashioned in my life for me and my brothers and sister.

Throughout my life my mother showed me unconditional, self-less love and support. Even during some of my darkest, saddest days of separation and divorce, mom was there to love and comfort me—even if she didn't agree with my decisions or my choices. She was there for me.

It's not hard to fashion a happy day in honor of the person who brought us into the world through her womb and raised us to adult hood through many turbulent times. I am sure there are times when because of my immature and selfish behavior my mother failed to like me or my behavior. I never doubted, though, that through it all she loved me unconditionally.

Toward the end of my mom's life—after a stroke took from her the ability to create her exquisite knitting and crocheting masterpieces—there were few days she would characterize as "happy days."

Living her life became a burden during her final days in the long term facility where she was confused and bedridden.

Her passing was a sad but "happy day." I believe she is in heaven with my father. I believe she is still connected with all four of us who had the honor of being her children. Such a belief makes this Mothers' Day an especially happy day for me to celebrate.

I also can celebrate this as a happy day because I know my wife Debby is safely beside her mother's side enjoying a sunny California day and preparing to bring her mom northward in a few days to spend time with us.

It is easy to fashion a positive perception out of a traditional holiday like mother's day.

It is almost as easy when it comes to celebrating the happy day occasion of a sibling's birthday.

14

Celebrating Sister"

Anytime I want to search my past for images and memories of people who brought joy and happiness into my life, I have to search no further than the memories I have about growing up with my sister Bonnie. The memories are fine medicine to take away any feelings or perceptions I have that might otherwise mire me down in a crappy day experience.

I chose to celebrate this happy day—May 3, 2010—by giving thanks for all the memories I have about Bonnie Jean Hite. Today is the occasion of her birthday. She is my older sister, but by not too many months. I will be 67 this September. Today she turns 68.

My sister now lives near Phoenix, Arizona with her husband Ken. I live in Eugene, Oregon with my wife Debby. It seems such a distance from when Bonnie and I were living with our folks in the tiny subdivision of

Rex Manor in the San Francisco Peninsula suburb of Mountain View.

I also have two brothers, Dennis and Larry, but due to the timing of my parent's family planning—or lack thereof—they were like the second phase of our family—as my sister and I were through almost a decade of life before Dennis appeared on the scene—and then still more years lapsed before Larry arrived.

With all respect to my two brothers, I confess when I think of growing up, I think the most about the adventures I had with my sister Bonnie. I am sure that Dennis and Larry have far more memories of their time together without having to share things with their sister and older brother.

Memories of the time with my sister make this an especially happy day. We had a delightful—some could say ideal—childhood because we were raised by a stay-at-home mother who dutifully fulfilled her obligations to serve as PTA room mother, Brownie and Girl Scout leader, and Den Mother for my Cub Scout pack.

My sister was the apple of my father's eye—though I don't think she felt that way when she hit her adolescence and started thinking she was far wiser than either of her parents. I shared her rebellion and we were probably the subject of many late night discussions between our frustrated and bewildered parents.

I was always proud of my sister—because she was my playmate and friend growing up—and because she was and is a very talented artist and creative person.

I am proud my sister was a popular cheerleader and song girl in high school. She was the beauty queen at our High School and was honored at Ms. Mountain View at the town's beauty pageant.

My sister and I both married—had two children—divorced and then re-married after long first marriages. I sometimes wonder if there wasn't something about the strange co-mingling of our genetic and our environmental upbringing that caused us both to suffer the same fate.

What memories do I recall most vividly about my sister as I celebrate her birthday with my happy dollar today?

I remember she loved to help me make popcorn when my folks went out for a few hours. She also could whip of a batch of fudge if given an hour to clean up the mess before mom got home. Somehow the fudge was never flaky but always gummy and we had to eat it out of the pan with a spoon.

I remember she backed my father's Buick under the flat-bed truck when they were making the senior float for the homecoming parade. It left a gaping gash in the trunk and Bonnie was petrified at the thought of owning up to the mishap! But dad understood and found a new trunk and repaired the car so it looked like new.

I remember she used to go to the pattern store and get a Simplicity pattern and material so she could make a new skirt or blouse. She loved clothes—especially in the 50s when angora sweaters were all the rage.

I remember she and I used to collect bottles from door-to-door solicitation in our neighborhood so we could buy fireworks for the Forth-of-July celebration. She loved to buy and burn the little black worms (they were called "snakes"). Dad hated them because they would leave a scar on the sidewalk that seemed to take a year to disappear regardless of what we used to clean the cement.

I remember my sister used to cringe when we would go weekly to the Saturday movies at the Mountain View Theatre—and I would sing the Star Spangled Banner or America the Beautiful in the intermission talent show. I remember, though, she would gladly take my victory spoils and head for the snack bar where she would return with an ABAZABA toffee bar that would last through the entire second movie of the double feature.

My sister and I loved living in the Santa Clara Valley and enjoyed all the fruit or the trees dad planted in the back yard. We used to compete to see who could find the reddest plumb and to shine its skin so it sparkled.

I most of all remember how much I enjoyed the fact that when she graduated from high school and started working for the phone company, my dad helped her buy a new Chevrolet Corvair—and how she reluctantly let me use it on special occasions for dates during my senior year of high school.

It has been a while since I last saw Bonnie in person—far too long. I am resolved on this happy day to find some time before this year is done to visit her in Arizona.

That's my happy dollar thought for today.

15

"Happy Monday?"

When you live a lifetime among those who worship the patterns and rituals of the culture of denial, you adopt many of the same habits—like hating Mondays and loving Fridays.   Why is either day more or less valuable than the other?

I suspect that try as we might, we are never going to popularize the expression, "Thank God it's Monday!"

In the culture of denial we learn to move quickly through stuff we don't like so we can get to the stuff we like. Mondays are the necessary vegetables of life's meal. Fridays are the desserts! Mondays focus us on returning to the challenges of the work week and all the stress it produces. Fridays focus us on all the diversions we enjoy on the weekend.

Like the face of living and the face of dying we see in the mirror each morning, both days are necessary to validate the value we place on the other. For most of us we will never learn how to put equal value on the inherent worth of these landmark days of the week. But we can work on it if we want to bring more balance into our outlook on life.

Today is May Monday. I was greeted by a rainy, overcast day this morning when I opened the front door and retrieved the newspaper from the green protective case located on the porch to the right of the door.

There is nothing inherently special about the day. No birthdays, no holidays to celebrate—nothing that I am especially looking forward to happening today.

In the past before I retired, when Monday morning arrived I usually stayed in bed until the last minute and then attacked the morning get-ready-for-work ritual with a vengeance. I hurried and made the bed, laid out my underwear and socks on the edge of the bed, then rushed to the bathroom where I quickly showered and shaved and returned to the bedroom to get dressed. I got so good at tying my necktie to the perfect length and with the tightest Windsor knot that I seldom had to consult with a mirror. I could complete the readiness ritual in slightly less than fifteen-minutes.

A few minutes later, after making coffee and toast and using one piece of toast to lure our two golden retrievers down the stairs and out the back yard into the fenced kennel for the day, I was behind the steering wheel of my car headed toward work.

Most of the time during the drive I was pre-occupied with thoughts about the challenges and issues I would face when I arrived at my office. I seldom thought about how I could celebrate the otherwise mundane reality of a Monday. I seldom took the time to enjoy the scenery as I wound my way through the surface streets through the Aptos Village and past the dozens of shops and businesses that dotted the street. Sadly, I was more preoccupied with how I was going to get through the day—and when I did, there would only be three more days until Friday—the day of the workweek that always seem joyful and special.

I confess that in retirement I still find it hard to think joyfully about the arrival of a Monday. It is still easier to feel more positive when Friday rolls around, although I was recently reminded by a friend who is still working a regular work week things are different for me. After our phone conversation he said to me, "Have a great weekend." He paused, and then added, "Oh I forgot, you're retired everyday is a weekend, isn't it!"

I wanted to assure him how I still suffered from the funk of mundane Mondays. It is still harder to craft a Happy Day perspective when it comes to Monday.

Today the only thing I have scheduled that will take me from my writing time in my study is a meeting I have this afternoon at one of the organizations where I volunteer my time as a board member. It is an obligation that will require me to dress up a bit from my normal casual sweats or jeans. I have to get in my car and drive a few miles that are outside of any normal Monday routine. It isn't something that I expect to look back on this evening and proclaim "that experience was the highlight of my Happy Monday."

So, here is the challenge we face in crafting Happy Day Mondays. We have to change our stereotype characterization of Monday. Use the backdrop of a Monday to remind ourselves of the precious gift we receive each day of the week.

Recall the Biblical scripture that proclaims, "This is the day the Lord had made, Rejoice in it!"

Instead of thinking of Monday as "mundane Monday" craft another metaphor. How about thinking of it as the "Gateway to the Work Week?" Is the concept "Magnificent Monday" too ostentatious? What about "Mellow Monday!"

If these images don't work and all else fails, return to the perspective that each day is a gift from the Lord, our creator. Regardless of which day of the calendar we are living, we need to take time to rejoice and find happiness in that day.

What am I celebration on this ordinary Monday that causes it to be my Happy Day?

This Monday I celebrate the pace of my life and how it has changed so much for the better since I entered retirement.

I still work—but for myself on what I want to do, not what someone else pays me to do. I don't feel compelled on this Monday to rush off into the routine of a workweek.

As an old track athlete, I no longer think of life in terms of "sprints" and "marathons." I think of the pace as a joyful 'fun run.' Now the pleasure of a Monday comes from just feeling good that I can still run the race—but at my pace.

It is my pace that allows me to celebrate this Monday as a Happy Day.

16

"The Mule-kicker"

I am blessed to have a few very special life-long friends still living and enjoying their senior years of life despite occasional brushes with death. I think our frequent conversations about aging, aches and pains, and worries about our health provide a bonding that helps us all focus on fashioning happy days with the time we have remaining.

One of my oldest friends—a college buddy who has stayed in touch over the years—Norman Page—the Mule-kicker is a good case in point.

My happy day dollar today is given in celebration of The Mule-kicker—a person who will soon arrive here in Eugene to spend some time with me attending the NCAA Track and Field Championships.

It is fitting that today is Cinco de Mayo—because Mexico is one of the Mule-kicker's favorite places to visit. He's fairly conversant in Spanish—and even has given a twist to his moniker by referring to himself as "el mulekickerdelsur."

The mule-kicker is one of those people who continue to help shape who I am through our decades of friendship.

I first met Norm when he appeared at my office door in Prince Lucien Campbell Hall at the University of Oregon. I still recall he was wearing a sports coat and necktie—and looked all together too well-groomed to be a graduate teaching assistant! I was a graduate-teaching fellow in my second year of graduate school. It was the fall of 1968—42 years ago. Unlike college friends who come and go Norm and I bonded and remained in touch over the years

He finished his Ph.D. a couple of years after I did and went to his first teaching job at Cal State University, Fullerton. He spent his entire career and is now in his early 70's and maintaining his emeritus professor status—teaching an occasional class and serving as a court mediator.

The mule-kicker moniker was his creation. When he would visit me and my family in Sacramento, he would pick up my five-year-old son Timothy by the legs and twirl him around—playfully calling him an "old mule-kicker." Somehow the term got associated with the image of "Uncle Norm" the mule-kicker.

Now the moniker has become our mutual term of endearment we call each other. We have always been there for each other in good and bad times. I spent time with Norm when my marriage ended—he was a good listener and knew enough to quietly support me during that turbulent time in my personal life.

He called me one evening almost a decade later and shared with me his angst over the news he had prostate cancer and needed an operation. That was the time in my life when I had moved into a new healthy relationship with Debby and enjoyed the companionship of her Golden Retriever, Buster.

To ease the mule-kicker through the recovery process I created my first book, **Buster at the Wall: A Golden Retriever looks at Life, Love, and Death.** He painted a canvas of Buster sitting next to me at the sea-wall where we went regularly to talk about stuff. It served as the cover for the book. We framed that canvas and it now hangs proudly over the bed in the upstairs bedroom we refer to as Norm's Room.

In addition to painting, Norm is a very talented craftsman who enjoys creating models of churches and old California missions and lighthouses. He recently started crafting his own home furniture—lamps and end tables and has done some excellent work.

The mule-kicker has visited us several times since we moved to Eugene a couple of years ago. When he visits we return to our old haunts at the University of Oregon campus and re-kindle old graduate school memories. I look forward to taking him to Taylor's for a beer and sandwich when he arrives this time. It is such a delight to look out the window from Taylor's and recalls our favorite stories of the old-days when we were graduate students crafting the education that became the foundation of our respective careers.

If I were looking for one word to associate with his name it would be this: Scrabble. The mule-kicker has a passion for scrabble. He also is quite good at the word game—given his knowledge of all the two-letter words that can build hefty scores. We have been known to go late into the evening with a game—and, I occasionally win one—but usually not.

Norm survived a heart attack a few years back—and had the traditional several graft by-pass surgery. He bounced back and continued on with his life—a reminder to me that we all have our health vulnerabilities. As I mentioned earlier, I also underwent a heart procedure in which my cardiologist inserted two tiny stents into my fully-occluded right coronary artery.

Norm has an independent spirit. He has never married and used to joke that he never dated a woman over thirty! Even though he had a string of relationships over the years, he seems quite content to remain a bachelor.

His spirit is inspiring. At age 70 he went out and bought a Vespa motor-scooter and joined a club of riders who get together for socializing and weekend rides. Even though he is currently having some idiopathic neurological issues that makes his lower extremities tingle with numbness, his zest and sparkle for life is a model I admire and respect. He doesn't let the small things slow him down!

Norm is eccentric when it comes to his automobiles. He prides himself in preserving each car so it is free of dings and scratches. I have walked great distances with him from his car to a restaurant or shopping center because he parks where no other vehicle will be able to put an unsightly ding into the flawless surface of his machine.

As the season heads toward summer we are both looking forward to his upcoming visit. This past New Years Day I drove to his place so we could attend the Rose Bowl Game—it was the second time Oregon's football team won the Pac-10 and the Bowl honor. We lost, but the trip to spend some time with "the mule-kicker" turned the event into a victory as far as I was concerned.

I'm certain he is going to relish the excitement of the four day NCAA Track Championships at Hayward Field.

I might even "let" him win a couple of scrabble games while he's here!

There is nothing more likely to transform an ordinary day into a happy day like connecting with an old friend—whether it is a lengthy phone call or an actual visit.

In the case of Norm it helps me validate that growing old and maturing is not something to dread, but to deal with joyfully the hands we are dealt and enjoy the happy days we share in friendship.

Or, to use a scrabble metaphor, to play the seven tiles we draw and to find "good words" as we craft each of our remaining happy days.

17

"A Lesson in Relationship"

In the recent weeks my heart has been heavy with feelings for my oldest friend and his now deceased wife, Joyce. Losing a spouse has got to be the toughest challenge in a person's life—regardless of when in life it happens.

Debby and I have spent many a recent evening discussing the reality that someday our relationship will face a similar fate.

Joyce's circumstances caused us to discuss openly how we will approach such a time when it presents itself to us. The situation our friends faced gave us the courage to step out of the normal boundaries of our culture of denial and talk openly about the eventuality of when our relation will end in death.

On the day Joyce died I knew there was a two-fold blessing on that day: Joyce was finally at peace in heaven; and, Lou was relieved of the tremendous weight of responsibility he felt to make his wife comfortable and at peace as she lived her final days as a human.

It is important to me that my relationship endures and strengthens with Lou as he moves on in his life's journey without Joyce.

I am choosing to celebrate this day's by putting a dollar into our Happy Day Dollar can in honor of my friendship with Lou.

The friendship I formed with Lou began a few years before he ever met Joyce. We were both undergraduates 46 years ago at Cal-State Hayward (Now East Bay University.)

We both ran on the cross-country team—neither of us were nationally-ranked runners—but were serious, disciplined runners who ran somewhere in the middle to top quartile of the pack. Lou was a tougher competitor than I was—perhaps because he was raised in a tough neighborhood in San Leandro.

I was an English/speech communication major. He was a physical education major with a passion for anatomy and physiology and a determination to become a professional in sports physiology. He was a senior my junior year. When I graduated and headed to the University of Oregon with a doctorate fellowship, he stayed at Cal-State Hayward and finished his Master's

Degree. Then, as fate would have it, he also found his way to Oregon's Doctorate program and we connected briefly during the last couple of years of my time at Oregon.

Lou is one of those rare people so respected as a student during his doctorate program that the University of Oregon recruited him back to its faculty after he did a short stint as an assistant professor at the University of Pacific in Stockton.

Unlike my pathway from a career in teaching at the university to a career as a hospital administrator, Lou prospered in his role as university faculty. He remained at the University of Oregon for his entire career until he retired professor emeritus a couple of years ago. He continues to maintain contact with his colleagues and associated at the university and is involved in grant research into the detection and treatment of concussions as sport's injuries.

At the time of his formal retirement, I received a call in my office at the hospital where I was COO. I hadn't hear his voice for well over a decade—but he was down in the Bay Area from Eugene and wanted to look me up and re-connect. We did. And, as it turned out, he was the key to my returning to Eugene.

Debby and I accepted his invitation to travel to Eugene and visit with Joyce and himself. We made the trip once and agreed to do it again the following fall during football season. On that second trip, the Sunday after the game (which Oregon lost to Cal due to a last minute goal-line fumble) Lou talked us into looking at a home that was the feature home on the Sunday Register-Guard real estate page.

We went to the open house and fell in love with the home and it location on the edge of Eugene/Junction City adjacent to a seasonal spring fed duck pond in our back yard. Before the trip was over we had become serious shoppers and looked at several other homes before confirming that the first home was the best. We drove back to Santa Cruz having put a down-payment on a new future in Eugene Oregon.

We put our Santa Cruz home on the market and on a rainy day the week before the Super Bowl in January we were on the road driving to our new home in Eugene.

Since we have returned to Eugene Lou and I have enjoyed attending track meets together at Hayward Field. The spring of our first year back in Eugene the University hosted the US Olympic Trials.

The track program that was a major focus during our graduate year's decades earlier had fallen on mediocre times for several years after the golden heydays of Bill Bowerman and his awesome teams. Fortunately, a couple of years before my return to Eugene, the university recruited a new coach who has re-built a powerhouse team and is once again a contender for national titles in track and field.

I relish going to meets with Lou. He knows so many folks and is a virtual encyclopedia about track history and lore at the University. As we watch the new spectacular athletes perform at Hayward Field, we are able to recall and re-savor the memories of those past running years when we were graduate students and could cheer for Steve Prefontaine, Roscoe Divine, Wade Bell, and dozens of other world-class athletes that made their way through the U of O during those golden days of Bowerman's rein as coach.

Lou still runs every day except Sundays—I go to the track several times a week for my two-three mile interval training, or a couple of mile loops around our neighborhood. Neither Lou nor I run in the age-groups of road races or toe up to the line of marathons these days. We are both in our mid-sixties and we both run alone these days—the fire of competition has been replaced by the tranquility of feeling blessed that we can still run and that we still enjoy time together.

It is comforting to know that a few miles is all the distance I now have to travel before I can enjoy a cup of coffee and conversation with a dear, old friend and fellow runner.

Now that Joyce is gone, I will make sure I continue with my friendship for Lou.

Perhaps, in God's Grand Design of Things, it was no coincidence that Debby and I moved to Eugene so we

could be here for Lou and a source of support and
fellowship in the years ahead.

18

"Landmark Days"

I am a disciplined keeper of a daily journal. I've maintained it for almost a decade. In recent years since we relocated to Oregon, I keep tabs on how many days we have enjoyed our new home in Eugene. I also keep track of how many days we have been blessed to enjoy our retirement. Today is Sunday, May 16, 2010. According to my journal it is our 834 day of Oregon and our 1726th day of retirement.

I made a quick calculation and realized that today is my 25,342 day of existence as a human—giving myself some margin for error for my failure to adjust for leap years over the past 66 years. If I live to my actuarial predicted age of death, that is 25 more years, or a total of 9,125 more days!

That is a sobering statistic. I've lived over 25 thousand days and have a much smaller number out on the horizon.

Of course all bets are off if God has different plans for when I am called home. But that is not something I need to worry about. When that day comes it most certainly will not be a "crappy day" by any stretch of the imagination.

One of the fun things I do to celebrate happy days is to take time out when I reach what I call a landmark day. I did so when we hit our first 100 days of Oregon. I also celebrate the anniversary of our first 1000 days of retirement.

There is nothing sacred or special about these days except from my healthy perspective. Many years ago when I was in graduate school I read a classic essay written by a prominent historian who proclaimed in the scholarly article title, "Everyman His Own Historian."

That concept stuck with me for some unexplainable reason—so much so that it popped into my mind as I was developing this essay. History is always dependent on the perspective of the historian—so when it comes to recording the history of our own life it is up to us to create the story we want told.

Each day we record through the events of our lives the history of one unique human being. It is a history we record through the eyes of the beholder. If we see it as filled with happy days and record it as such, then contrary to anyone else's views of our time on earth, we write the history of a happy person. If we see our history filled with crappy days, then regardless of how others see our time and accomplishments, we write a crappy history.

History seems more readable when there are boundaries and landmarks that create beginning and end points. In the history of our time as a human there are the bookend landmarks of Birth and Death. But if we are conscientious personal historians, we have the obligation to identify and celebrate landmarks along the way.

Birthdays are the most notable landmark days—and even for the non-historian, there is the time-out to pause and celebrate such points along the journey. But if all we do is track our landmark birthdays, we are missing a lot of opportunities to celebrate happy day occasions that fall between the "big 30, 40, 50, 60, and the big 70 that I am still a few yearss away from celebrating!

That's why I created the Oregon data and the retirement data. These two frames of reference provide me with a whimsical opportunity to celebrate whenever the mood strikes me. I will surely point out to my wife Debby the morning when we hit the anniversary of our 1000 day of Oregon. I will find some way to celebrate when we hit our 2000 day of retirement, as well.

I'm not sure why it is the case, but historians seem to like the round numbers. They like to divide history into decades and centuries. When it comes to evaluating a new president, the first 100 and first 1000 days have become the frame of reference.

My point in raising this perspective is to encourage folks to create their own historical frame of references and use them as a guidepost for celebrating landmarks along their own historical journey.

Why? Because each of us is living our history a day at a time. Each of us is capable of recording our days as insignificant in our frame of reference, or more significant.

I enjoy celebrating landmark along the journey. I like stuffing a dollar into our happy dollar container and celebrating the landmark I created as the basis for a happy day.

A healthy perspective is dependent on each of us to take very seriously the responsibility to be our own historian.

19

"Things We Take for Granted"

Almost by definition, the things we take for granted are seldom the cause to pause and push a happy dollar into a container and proclaim them the subject of a daily celebration.

We certainly take good health and our sensory faculties for granted until one malfunctions—then we show concern and can worry, leading to a preoccupation that otherwise might end up causing a crappy day.

And in addition to taking health for granted until something fails, there are countless other things in life we have come to expect and therefore take off our daily screen of things to celebrate and give thanks for their existence.

This morning when I was walking through our neighborhood and enjoying a cup of coffee and the solitude of a sunny day walk I decided to make a mental list of the things I take for granted each day. My hope was such a thoughtful activity would provide me with a renewed list of things I might pause and celebrate with future happy dollars.

Here's the list:

I take for granted that I am an American and I live in a democratic country.

I take for granted that I have the basic freedoms guaranteed by our constitution and the bill of rights.

I take for granted that I have freedom of speech and the freedom to express an unpopular view without fear of reprisal.

I take for granted that I live in a peaceful, beautiful little neighborhood in Eugene, Oregon.

I take for granted it is safe and secure to walk on the streets and not be subjected to crime and violence.

I take for granted the infrastructure of the services the government provides the people of our community through the responsible use of our tax dollars.

I take for granted there will be food on my table and clothes on my back.

When I say I take something for granted that means I expect it to be present in the world around me—it doesn't mean I don't appreciate and am thankful for such conditions. It does mean, however, that I seldom spend much time or awareness on these everyday realities.

This list makes me aware of how awesome the operations of our democratic society work in providing for the common welfare. I am not someone who resents paying taxes for public schools and public services— though I get annoyed when I hear of foolish, wasteful government spending. That's when I use my ballot to raise such objections.

When I hear the far-left and far-right political fringes express inflammatory rhetoric aimed at alarming folks that our basic way of life is being eroded I smile and do not take for granted that such expressions are themselves evidence of how our way of government works.

I am proud to be an American and I am proud to live in our Democratic society. When all else fails to transform an otherwise crappy day view into a happy day, don't forget to pause and give thanks for all it means to live in this freedom loving, diverse American culture. The thought should bring a smile to your face. It might even cause you to get out the American flag stored in your garage and display it proudly on days other than The Fourth-of-July!

20

"Preparing for the Death of Our Dog"

It is Monday, May 18, 2010. We are taking our precious Golden Retriever Luke to see the vet this afternoon. It may well be we will decide to have the vet put him to sleep! It will be a challenge not to call this a crappy day if that decision is made.

Luke's health has been failing, but he had until most recently lived a happy, vital more than twelve years—which is old for a large retriever. He has some cancerous tumors on his rear legs and they often come out from under him at unexpected times on our walks. I watch the concerned look on Debby's face as she examines Luke's drooping eye and observes he is having difficulty chewing his food.

As I sit at my computer keyboard and look through my study door I see Luke lying peaceful on the cool tile of our entryway. That is where he spends much of his time these days. I think he is not in pain or suffering—he is just old and getting more feeble each day.

To help me through the sadness of Luke's final day, I recently wrote a poem and posted it on our pantry bulletin board. This morning I took it down and brought it into my study to remind me that even in moments of sadness and grief, we can find strength and support. It is possible to find peace if today turns out to be that final day.

Here is the poem:

When It is Time

No human knows when it's his "time."

God's messenger comes like a "thief in the night."

A loving God knows when a human's transforming time is right.

With dogs such reasoning is left behind.

We serve God's purpose by knowing when to unleash a dog's spirit from failing flesh.

The decision's our final test.

Did we learn the lesson of unconditional love our dog spent his life time teaching?

We've selfishly enjoyed a dog's companionship— ignoring the reality of the "it's time" message we'd soon be preaching.

*We now prepare in sunlight hours to selflessly bestow
our loving gift upon our friend.*

*It's comforting to believe our dog-child transforms and
cavorts again*

In metaphorical fields of heavenly peace and thrives.

We grieve with loving tears as his time arrives.

We will not, however, grieve our decision.

*We will, instead, relish memories he fashioned for us in
bit size bits of daily love.*

God gives angels to direct us from above.

He gives us a dog to teach us lessons of love.

*We can share no greater love for our dog than knowing
when it's time.*

When it's time

Our decision is the ultimate test of unconditional love.

In rereading this poem it occurs to me that a sad day is different than a crappy day. Sad things happen in the course of our life's journey. Nothing can transform the sadness of losing a friend to death into a happy day.

I prepare myself for the sadness by calling into the present moment the memories of Luke's happy times when our other now-deceased golden Toby carried Luke by the back of his neck and mothered him as an infant puppy. Twelve years of happy memories will help me deal with the sadness and prevent it from becoming a crappy day.

The abundance of happy memories will grant me the peace to overcome my sadness and continue on with my own remaining days.

Post-script: The vet advised us that Luke's eye is not a source of any pain to him and his quality of life is not suffering beyond the typical infirmaries of old-age. We were relieved to hear there are a few more happy days with Luke ahead—days we will cherish one day at a time!

Post-post-script: We finally took our beloved Luke to the vet and ushered him off to a better place. It was our gift to him for being a loving pet for all these years. We were sad, but somehow the death of our friend Joyce helped us cope with the responsibility of putting down Luke.

I think there was a strange bonding that happened between Luke and Joyce during the last visit she and Lou made to our home. After dinner Luke wandered into the dining room in search of morsels of food and attention. Both Lou and Joyce were aware Luke was on his last legs. She seemed to be so understanding of his condition and so tender in her affection toward him that evening.

I like to think Joyce is now joyfully taking care of Luke until we arrive someday in the future. I think she will.

21

"Our Hour Upon the Stage"

"Life is but a poor fool that struts and frets its hour upon the stage then is heard no more"—thus concludes the Bard in one of his famous passages. We all have a fleeting moment of time in God's Grand Scheme of things to perform our part in an awesome plan.

There is no dress rehearsal, no opportunity to practice our lines or our stage movements. Whether we like it or not, our time is brief and our part pre-determined before we are born.

I recently took to heart the metaphor Herman Wouk expands upon in his book, THE LANGUAGE GOD TALKS. He mentions how the universe appears to be such a large stage in which to set the drama of any battle between good and evil. The cynical and agnostic view holds that the stage is too big and unnecessary for such acting out the history or humanity and its struggle to overcome evil with goodness. Why did God need such an awesome collection of universes that seem ever expanding beyond the tiny planet we occupy in this galaxy known as "the Milky Way?"

I have tried to put my understanding of God's Grand Design of Things into the stage perspective. Here we have the planet Earth—our stage—populated with somewhere around 6 billion people—each soul occupying a tiny role and some not having any speaking part at all. We have all the human drama of natural tragedies, wars and famines and diseases afflicting those who populate this tiny blue marble theatre in the round.

A handful of actors leave marks sufficient that their passing makes the evening news—head of states, famous actors, famous athletes, and famous creative artists.

None of us will ever see God's play in all its epic proportions from the moment of the Big Bang creation through the final death throes of our mighty universe that contains planet Earth. Scientists speculate when and how this end will come—religious prophets give us indications of how Christ will one day return to Earth and wrap of the play as though some cosmic stage manager speaking a voice over and wrapping up loose ends.

When I try to perceive the vastness of our cosmic stage, I can't help recalling the classic Thornton Wilder's play; OUR TOWN when the stage manager transcends the stage action and enables us to perceive how the frail human existence in one tiny community becomes a metaphor for God's cosmic drama.

Sometimes I wonder who is the audience of this global theatre and from where do they observe the action? Did God create the drama of Good versus Evil just for his own entertainment? Do all the actors who have played their part become some heavenly audience?

If the giant blue marble of this Earthly stage is sufficient to contain all the life God had created, then it would seem there is merit to the charge that the whole stage of the universe is far too vast a creation for housing the mere drama of human existence.

I wonder if in ancient times the early humans were not in a better place when it came to understanding the nature of the human condition. It must have been comforting to think that there was a heaven above earth and a fiery pit of hell under the ground where evil resided. It must have been comforting to think the earth was flat and was the center of the universe.

Now look at all we know about creation and the vastness of the cosmos and how tiny the Earth is in the awesome expanding cosmos God created in the beginning.

What challenges my faith is the belief that the Earthly life drama of God's creatures is one in which each actor has a personal connection to the playwright. I find it impossible to understand such a condition—but trust that just as I feel connected in my own prayerful relationship with Jesus, other believers feel a similar connection.

I don't think we are helping God write the script as we pray for his interventions and his blessings—the script has already been written and when we ask for modification they occur only because we were supposed to ask and interact with the Creator.

In the final analysis, I don't have to understand the plot of the play. I just have to be thankful I have been given a part and enjoy the happy day time I have on the stage.

22

"Doesn't Sweat the Small Stuff!"

It is Wednesday, May 19th and my happy day celebration dollar is offered in recognition of a special friend and former colleague Lee Vanderpool. He is one of the most optimistic and level-headed people I have the opportunity to work with in my professional career.

Lee still works at Dominican Hospital where he was a vice-president on the senior management team I headed as the hospital's Chief Operations Officer.

Lee was a champion of our hospital's quality improvement efforts. He appropriately characterized himself as "the designated worrier" about all the details that need to be attended to in our organization's efforts to achieve recognition as a national role model for quality in health care services.

I still find it ironic that Lee championed the expression, "Don't Sweat the Small Stuff—and remember, everything is small stuff! I learned over the years, however, that "worry" wasn't a negative concept in Lee's perspective. He didn't wring his hands when he "worried." Worry meant intense focus and attention to detail. It meant never dropping the ball or failing to cross all the T's and dot the I's in any report or document that bore his name.

One of the things I learned about Lee was that never in his life did he ever have a physical fist fight with anybody—not even when he was a kid growing up in a tough neighborhood in the city of Richmond, California. How many people can make such a claim? I certainly had more than my share of black eyes for mouthing off at the wrong time to the bully in the various neighborhoods where I lived as a child.

Perhaps his even-keel disposition was a function of the fact he had a congenital heart problem that resulted in a childhood open-heart surgery to correct the problem. They did the best they could with the technology of the time, but the root-cause of his weak heart was undetected until this year when he turned 60.

When a new CEO was hired to head the hospital's senior management team many of the vice-presidents that worked well as colleagues on my leadership team were let go and replaced with a new senior team. Lee's VP role was eliminated and because of his expertise in Hospital Information Systems, he was offered a less high profile job as a Senior Director rather than a Vice President.

It speaks volumes that nowhere in the turmoil and disruption of such monumental career altering changes did Lee act in anything but a professional manner. He literally didn't sweat the small stuff! He simply made the best of a difficult transition and moved into his new role with the same vitality and determination to succeed he had in his former role.

A mid-afternoon health crisis occurred in his office where he found himself suffering from some unexplainable double vision. When it didn't immediately disappear, he walked over to the emergency room where he was checked out in an effort to rule-out a TIA or a mini-stroke. The episode connected him with one of the outstanding cardiologist on the hospital staff, Dr. Raj Singh. Dr. Singh was my personal hero from several years earlier when he detected blockage in my right coronary artery and inserted two tiny stents that opened the 100% occluded artery. He literally saved my life and prevented the inevitable sudden death heart attack that was lurking on my horizon.

Dr. Singh performed a similar miracle for Lee Vanderpool. He elected to do one additional test in his effort to uncover the cause of Lee's health problem. The positive test results sent Lee to Stanford Hospital where he was presented to the head of the cardiac transplant services. The world-famous surgeon was amazed at the complexity of Lee's dysfunctional heart. Fortunately, he made several major repairs. When the surgery was over the team of physicians exclaimed that the positive outcome actually helped Lee dodge not one fatal bullet, but FOUR!

So, instead of writing this chapter in the form of an obituary and eulogy, I write it as a celebration of the continuing health and vitality of a dear friend I have admired for over twenty five years!

In a few months, at the end of summer Lee and his wife Johna will fly to Eugene to attend a football game with us and to journey down to Ashland to see a Shakespeare play.

So, today I build my happy day perception around celebrating the continuing friendship I enjoy with Lee and the anticipation I have for when we will be together enjoying each other company in the future.

It is nice to know that the champion of "Don't Sweat the Small Stuff" is enjoying his family and relishing the time he spends with his friends and colleagues at work.

Staying in contact with Lee through e-mail and occasional face-to-face visits enriches my life and reminds me that the truly meaningful things in life grow from relationships, not things or accomplishments.

23

"Anticipating Future Happy Days"

I appreciate the philosophy that we only have the present day and should find our sources of happiness in today. I also have come to appreciate that there is nothing wrong with enjoying as a part of this day's celebration the joy of anticipating a future event we are looking forward to experiencing.

Today I intend to be mindful of how joyful it is to plan and anticipate happy times that will occur in the future. I give thanks to God the creator of this day that I can be optimistic and look with anticipation to future happy days.

There are a whole bunch of things we have penciled into our calendar that I am looking forward to enjoying. I am looking forward to this July when my son and daughter-in-law will bring our twin grandsons to Oregon for a visit. I look forward to the possibility my youngest son and his wife will also visit during that same period. In August I look forward to participating in the graduation ceremony of the small private university in Provo, Utah where I am a new member of the Board of Trustees. At the end of summer I am looking forward to a visit from my friend Lee and his wife Johna. Then, mid-way through September I am looking forward to a trip to Hawaii with Debby and my mother-in-law Verla. After that my friend Norm will return to watch a football game with me at Autzen stadium.

All that could change and not come to pass—because there are no guarantees there will be that many tomorrows on my horizon. But that reality is outside of my control and is appropriately in the hands of God.

I think it is healthy for us to anticipate positive things we look forward to in the future. Imagine how sad it would be if we only focused on negative things that we didn't look forward to occurring in the future. That's what a pessimist would be inclined to do and it would be in the form of worry and anxiety.

Just like we can create a crappy day vision of the current day instead of seeing the things that are present that transform the day into a happy day, we can have the same phenomena operating on how we view the future.

A pessimist can and often does create a negative map of a future territory that doesn't exist. The pessimist can fill the future calendar with worries about failing health conditions, and a host of other things to worry about.

Such worry and grief about things that are yet to happen add to the dark clouds of gloom that gather over our unhealthy perception of the current day and contribute to its crappiness.

Looking forward should not be an escape from the responsibility of crafting a happy vision of all that exists in this current day, but it should help reinforce a person's general outlook that life is good and it holds the potential to get even better as more days unfold into the future.

My father was a Nebraska stoic farm boy who grew up believing that if we ever let on that we were enjoying the present day too much or looking forward with anticipation toward a bright future, then the other-shoe would fall and our prideful joy would be squashed by the reality of bad things happening. It was best to not get to excited or joyful but to just accept things as they happen—the good and the bad. Otherwise, we would be tempting fate by showing how happy we were with how things were going in our lives.

I think there are a lot of people who go through life sharing the perspective I saw in my father. It is a reflection of humility and a fear that things will be taken away if we get carried away with expecting good things to continue to happen in our lives.

Celebrating happiness for many can be viewed as tempting fate—if it looks like we expect good things in the future we are not being humble and are expecting more good things.

It may come down to the way we perceive many of the Biblical lessons we were taught about the story of Job. If we are joyful about our blessings then maybe God will test us by taking away the blessings and seeing if we maintain our faith in the light of lack of a continual flow of happy days and a bright future.

Don't be too optimistic about the blessings of the current day or expect too much by anticipating a bright future filled with more of God's abundance. If you are, then you might get singled out for the test of your faith. Keep a low profile and don't publically display joyful celebration. Be thankful and humble. Don't run the risk of being perceived by God as prideful and greedy for still more of a good thing.

Today I enrich my happy day by being mindful of many of the future happy day activities I anticipate enjoying in my future. The possibility of these events happening is a source of joy today.

Today I celebrate being optimistic about my future and humble in realizing that such future blessings are outside my control.

Today I give myself permission to create in my mind's eye a positive perception of a future. I know it is only the fantasy of my imagination that will be delighted by such a picture. I know it isn't a reality and may never become a reality. But I will continue to paint the canvas of my future with positive images of happy events and joyful experiences.

24

"Flashbulb Memories"

My friend Bob Welch is a talented newspaper columnist and published author of several well-written books. One of his recent columns introduced me to the metaphor of how our lives contain what he called "flashbulb memories." He was referring to the memories that are indelibly etched forever in the archives of our personal history—memories that seemed to mark the big moments in our brief time upon the stage of life.

Today I celebrate how my archives of flashbulb memories allows me to enjoy the richness of my current days whenever I take time out to ask myself, "Where were you when _____ happened?

Such a thoughtful personal journey through our times will produce a different set of experiences and reveal fragments of our own place on the stage when the flashbulb event of history occurred.

Where were you on 911? I was in Munich at a hotel in a predominantly Muslim part of the city. We had just come back from dinner at the famous Hofbrau House and I sat in disbelief as I watched the image of two airplanes crash into the side of the Twin Towers. I watched as the buildings crumbled down and people jumped to their death from the burning buildings.

Where were you when President Kennedy was shot? I was in a Shakespeare class at Foothill College. The teacher announced the tragedy and then opened our textbook and read these famous lines from a speech about the death of Percy Hotspur: "When this body held a spirit, the entire world could not contain it. Now, two paces of the vilest earth are enough!" He shut the book and dismissed class. I will forever link that passage with the President's death and the stunned world I was a part of that day.

Where were you when Princess Diane was killed? We were in Maui and were celebrating my wife Debby's birthday when we saw the news on the television.

Where were you when the American's landed on the Moon? I was in Germany with my former wife and toddler son Timothy. I remember seeing the German Newspapers and the headlines, "DER ALDER IST GELANDED! The eagle has landed.

Where were you when Robert Kennedy was killed? I was asleep on the couch in our apartment in Eugene Oregon. Earlier in the day I had attended the rally for him on downtown Willamette Street. I remember watching in disbelief as football player Rosie Greer wrestled the assassin to the ground.

Where were you when the Loma Prieta Earthquake hit the San Francisco Bay Area? I was in the administrative offices at Dominican Hospital talking to my secretary Rosemary Stewart—as the quake intensified I watched her crawl under her desk as I stood in the doorway. I still recall the pavement under my feet rolling like it was a piece of carpet as the aftershocks hit the front of the hospital where I was gathered with the management team to develop our disaster response.

It is interesting that these are the flashbulb moments that immediately came to my mind as I rummaged through my own memory archives. There are surely other events that will occur to me as I continue writing this book.

I wonder how many more flashbulb memories will be recorded in my life as I continue through the final days of my brief moment on the stage of the epic history of my time.

Today, however, I celebrate these flashbulb moments and appreciate they are part of the rich human history I am bless to enjoy in my happy days as a human.

25

"If You Still Can't 'See Happy'"

I hope that by this point readers are realizing that all this talking about death has involved talking equally about happy day experiences being fashioned despite the acknowledgement and acceptance of the ever-present face of death in our lives.

It can be healthy to step outside the culture of denial that surrounds us and talk openly and positively about the ever presence of death in our lives. Living and dying are occurring simultaneously in our lives. Acknowledge both and focus on creating a balanced healthy day perspective. It is the best medicine to treat any of the discomfort brought on by the crappy things that can happen along the journey.

At the end of each day it is going to be up to us to declare we saw it as a happy day.

If you still can't "see happy" after reading this series of reflections, then here is where we part ways. I can't make you see happy. It is up to you. God created each of us in his likeness. God didn't tell each of us what we were going to receive as we undertook our mortal journey. God did, however, give each of us control over our beliefs, attitudes, and perceptions.

I have tried to show how we can live a rich life filled with happy day perceptions if we choose to enjoy the control God gave us over how we perceive the drama of life as it unfolds for us.

If you are caught up in anger, resentment, hostility, and disappointment that God did not deal you a "happy hand" in the poker game of life, then there is nothing more I can offer you.

If you think you were dealt a bad hand, then you are going to see life as crappy and not happy. Despite the insights I have tried to provide through these reflections, you will feel you've been screwed.

Life sucks. It is not fair. God dealt you a bad hand.

O.K. Let's suppose God did!

Now what?

Let's suppose you are approaching the end of your mortal time upon this awesome stage of human life.

Let's suppose you are facing your mortality.

Those among us who are happiest on this day and those who feel the day is crappy will all eventually face the reality of the fact that our life will end.

Life is an epic journey that continues on a day at a time. We are all going to die. That is a fact we don't celebrate in each of our happy day celebrations!

How can we celebrate "seeing happy" when we know how the play is destined to end?

It takes great courage to live each of our happy days with the knowledge we are mortal. We were created by God to grow, mature, and die.

We will all die.

That is a reality.

Somewhere along the journey we need to learn to see our demise as a happy day. That is the greatest challenge we face as mortals.

We are mortal. We will all pass from this stage of our human drama. We will speak our lines and be gone.

That is a part in the play we don't like to acknowledge.

However, there is an option—and it has to deal with the great gift God gave us to use in our daily journey. We are in control of our beliefs, our attitudes, and our perceptions.

Take charge, fellow humans.

Carpe Diem! Seize the day. You are in charge of your happy days.

Awake each morning and give thanks you are alive. Give prayerful petitions to God for what you want from the day.

Step from the bed sheets to the day and revel in all that God challenges you with in the day.

When your head returns to your pillow in the evening, give thanks that you have been gifted another of God's day.

You do not get out of life alive—your facilities will diminish. You will not grow stronger over the years. You will feel your life is weakened.

The challenge, though, is to maintain the raging passion of squeezing the last drip of life and vitality from your journey.

As a runner I used to watch inexperienced young athletes finish a long race with a burst of speed that told their coaches they had a lot left in their "gas tank." Life you life so that at the end the tank is empty. Don't leave any fuel in the tank. Be exhausted.

The prize at the end of life's marathon is the gold of every-lasting life for all eternity.

Only then will the face of death forever disappear from your countenance.

Until that happy day, rejoice in all the remaining days God gives you and enjoy the challenge of balancing the reality of life and death by transforming each day into a happy day!

26

"A Final 'Good Word' about Death"

My wife Debby and I talked a lot in the days following the death of our friend.

Like the peasant who was curious about how the frightened prince felt when he faced death, Debby and I talked about how our friend and her husband felt in those final days. We wondered if the many months of the battle with cancer somehow prepared them for the final days. We wondered if in some strange way there was relief on both of their parts that the struggle was over. We wondered how long it would take before our friend could feel a sense of peace even though his wife was no longer at his side?

It was sobering talk—talk about how we would want things when it comes time for each of us to put our house in order and prepare for death.

We both said that when our time comes, we wanted a memorial service so our friends could celebrate our life and bring closure to their relationship with each of us.

We both agree that we will be cremated and then buried in the plot Debby purchased a few years ago in the cemetery where her dad is buried on Paradise, CA.

Debby said that when her times comes she would like to write a personal letter that could be sent after her death to our close friends summarizing what she wanted her friends to know about the time leading up to her death. It would be a more personal way of saying goodbye and getting closure for her and hopefully for her friends as well. If she died before me, she felt a letter might also ease the burden on me to communicate news of her death to those who are a part of our network of family and friends.

In the days immediately after Joyce's death, I felt a heavy heart and sadness for my friend Lou. I thought back at how I babbled some words of condolence on the phone that afternoon when he shared with me the news of Joyce's death. Words seemed so useless in conveying my feelings—but that was all I could share.

I thought about all the dizzying details involved in taking care of her funeral and burial. It made my stomach queasy. I didn't sleep well the night I learned of Joyce's death. I wondered how Lou would feel falling asleep knowing Joyce was no longer alive in their home. I tried to imagine the positive and thought about how after so many weeks of worry and concern it might be the first peaceful sleep for him as well.

I have to admit I felt foolish trying to imagine what it was like. It was, however, impossible to get such thought out of my mind. I tried to imagine if I were dealing with Debby's death how would I cope.

I finally retreated to the safety of our culture of denial and took a deep breath, "Time to stop dwelling upon such unpleasant thought. Be thankful it wasn't my time—this time."

But if it were my time—I continued to imagine—what did I want to have said at my own memorial service? I don't mean the list of my accomplishments or the recollection of stories about my life. Instead, I wanted people to understand how I viewed my own death. I wanted them to know I had grown comfortable with the reality and did not see death as something negative.

I recalled an aphorism I wrote in a collection several years ago:

"Death is a friendship that requires a lifetime to appreciate."

That pretty much sums up my perspective. We spend a lifetime with something we don't place much value or worth upon until the very end. In the final analysis, death is a friend.

I hope this collection of essays and reflections provides a resource for people to appreciate my perspective about death.

I am a Christian who views death as the transition between this life and eternal life. I believe it is through the grace of God—not my personal deeds and accomplishments—that will allow me safe passage to the place our theology calls heaven.

As I said at the beginning of these reflections, I believe the final good word about death is that it is the moment when we receive a gift greater than the awesome gift God gave us when we were born into human life.

The good word is "peace."

Death is peace—and a new beginning in which there is no end!

Debby and I are more determined than ever to relish each of our remaining days and to enjoy all the blessing we have been given.

It time to buy some more green bananas and to spread the good word—"peace."

Made in the USA
Charleston, SC
19 April 2014